P9-CMW-249

Teach Yourself
VISUALLY™
Word 2007

Visual

by Elaine J. Marmel

BICENTENNIAL
1807
WILEY
2007
BICENTENNIAL

Wiley Publishing, Inc.

Teach Yourself VISUALLY™ Word 2007

Published by
Wiley Publishing, Inc.
111 River Street
Hoboken, NJ 07030-5774

Published simultaneously in Canada

Library of Congress Control Number: 2006934806

ISBN-13: 978-0-470-04593-0

ISBN-10: 0-470-04593-0

Manufactured in the United States of America

10 9 8 7 6 5 4 3 2 1

Trademark Acknowledgments

Contact Us

For general information on our other products and services please contact our Customer Care Department within the U.S. at 800-762-2974, outside the U.S. at 317-572-3993, or fax 317-572-4002.

For technical support please visit www.wiley.com/techsupport.

Wiley Publishing, Inc.

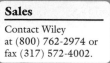

Sales

Contact Wiley
at (800) 762-2974 or
fax (317) 572-4002.

Praise for Visual Books

"Like a lot of other people, I understand things best when I see them visually. Your books really make learning easy and life more fun."

John T. Frey (Cadillac, MI)

"I have quite a few of your Visual books and have been very pleased with all of them. I love the way the lessons are presented!"

Mary Jane Newman (Yorba Linda, CA)

"I just purchased my third Visual book (my first two are dog-eared now!), and, once again, your product has surpassed my expectations."

Tracey Moore (Memphis, TN)

"I am an avid fan of your Visual books. If I need to learn anything, I just buy one of your books and learn the topic in no time. Wonders! I have even trained my friends to give me Visual books as gifts."

Illona Bergstrom (Aventura, FL)

"Thank you for making it so clear. I appreciate it. I will buy many more Visual books."

J.P. Sangdong (North York, Ontario, Canada)

"I have several books from the Visual series and have always found them to be valuable resources."

Stephen P. Miller (Ballston Spa, NY)

"Thank you for the wonderful books you produce. It wasn't until I was an adult that I discovered how I learn – visually. Nothing compares to Visual books. I love the simple layout. I can just grab a book and use it at my computer, lesson by lesson. And I understand the material! You really know the way I think and learn. Thanks so much!"

Stacey Han (Avondale, AZ)

"I absolutely admire your company's work. Your books are terrific. The format is perfect, especially for visual learners like me. Keep them coming!"

Frederick A. Taylor, Jr. (New Port Richey, FL)

"I have several of your Visual books and they are the best I have ever used."

Stanley Clark (Crawfordville, FL)

"I bought my first Teach Yourself VISUALLY book last month. Wow. Now I want to learn everything in this easy format!"

Tom Vial (New York, NY)

"Thank you, thank you, thank you...for making it so easy for me to break into this high-tech world. I now own four of your books. I recommend them to anyone who is a beginner like myself."

Gay O'Donnell (Calgary, Alberta, Canada)

"I write to extend my thanks and appreciation for your books. They are clear, easy to follow, and straight to the point. Keep up the good work! I bought several of your books and they are just right! No regrets! I will always buy your books because they are the best."

Seward Kollie (Dakar, Senegal)

"Compliments to the chef!! Your books are extraordinary! Or, simply put, extra-ordinary, meaning way above the rest! THANK YOU THANK YOU THANK YOU! I buy them for friends, family, and colleagues."

Christine J. Manfrin (Castle Rock, CO)

"What fantastic teaching books you have produced! Congratulations to you and your staff. You deserve the Nobel Prize in Education in the Software category. Thanks for helping me understand computers."

Bruno Tonon (Melbourne, Australia)

"Over time, I have bought a number of your 'Read Less - Learn More' books. For me, they are THE way to learn anything easily. I learn easiest using your method of teaching."

José A. Mazón (Cuba, NY)

"I am an avid purchaser and reader of the Visual series, and they are the greatest computer books I've seen. The Visual books are perfect for people like myself who enjoy the computer, but want to know how to use it more efficiently. Your books have definitely given me a greater understanding of my computer, and have taught me to use it more effectively. Thank you very much for the hard work, effort, and dedication that you put into this series."

Alex Diaz (Las Vegas, NV)

Credits

Project Editors
Sarah Hellert
Maureen Spears

Acquisitions Editor
Jody Lefevere

Product Development Supervisor
Courtney Allen

Copy Editor
Scott Tullis

Technical Editor
Diane Koers

Editorial Manager
Robyn Siesky

Editorial Assistant
Laura Sinise

Business Manager
Amy Knies

Manufacturing
Allan Conley
Linda Cook
Paul Gilchrist
Jennifer Guynn

Book Design
Kathie Rickard

Production Coordinator
Adrienne Martinez

Layout
Jennifer Mayberry
Heather Ryan

Screen Artist
Jill A. Proll

Illustrators
Ronda David-Burroughs
Cheryl Grubbs
Joyce Haughey
Jacob Mansfield

Proofreader
Evelyn Still

Quality Control
Christy Pingleton

Indexer
Johnna VanHoose

Vice President and Executive Group Publisher
Richard Swadley

Vice President and Publisher
Barry Pruett

Composition Director
Debbie Stailey

About the Author

Elaine Marmel is president of Marmel Enterprises, LLC, an organization that specializes in freelance technical writing and software training. Elaine has an MBA from Cornell University and has worked on projects to build financial management systems in New York City and Washington, D.C. Elaine spends most of her time writing; since 1994, she has been a contributing editor to monthly magazines *Peachtree Extra* and *QuickBooks Extra*. She co-wrote *Peachtree For Dummies, 2nd Edition* (Wiley, 2004), and wrote *Microsoft Office Project 2003 Bible* (Wiley, 2003), *Master VISUALLY Project 2003* (Wiley, 2004), and *Master VISUALLY QuickBooks 2005* (Wiley, 2005), and she has authored and coauthored more than 30 other books.

Although a native of Chicago, Elaine has seen much of the world, including Cincinnati, Ohio; Jerusalem, Israel; Ithaca, New York; Washington, D.C., and Tampa, FL. As of this writing, she has settled into a perfect house in Arizona, and lives with her purrfect cats, Cato, Watson, and Buddy (who seems to be made of velcro, sticking to Elaine when she starts to write), and her doting and loving dog, Josh (who watches the door for visitors and may lick you to death while performing the job of general welcoming committee).

Author's Acknowledgments

Nobody writes a book alone; every book is the combined effort of many people. I'd like to thank Jody Lefevere for giving me the opportunity to write this book; Maureen Spears for once again making the process painless; Sarah Hellert for picking up the slack at the appropriate moment; Scott Tullis for making me look good; and Diane Koers for her keen eye in keeping me technically accurate. Thanks also to the graphics and production teams who labor tirelessly behind the scenes to create the elegant appearance of this book.

Dedication

To Gayle Kearney, a true friend

Table of Contents

 **chapter 1**   A First Look at Word

 **chapter 2**   Managing Documents

chapter 3 Edit Text

Table of Contents

chapter **6** Format Paragraphs

Table of Contents

chapter 7 Format Pages

chapter 8 Print Documents

chapter 9

Create Tables and Charts

Table of Contents

chapter **10**   **Work With Graphics**

chapter **11**   **Customize Word**

chapter 12 Work with Mass Mailing Tools

chapter 13 Word and the Internet

How to Use This Book

Do you look at the pictures in a book or newspaper before anything else on a page? Would you rather see an image instead of read about how to do something? Search no further. This book is for you. Opening *Teach Yourself VISUALLY Word 2007* allows you to read less and learn more about Word 2007.

Who Needs This Book

This book is for a reader who has never used this particular technology or software application. It is also for more computer literate individuals who want to expand their knowledge of the different features that Word 2007 has to offer.

Book Organization

Teach Yourself VISUALLY Word 2007 is divided into 13 chapters, each of which teaches you a specific Word 2007 topic.

Chapter 1, **A First Look at Word**, covers Word basics, including an overview of the Word Window, how to enter text, and how to use the menus, toolbars, and task panes.

Chapter 2, **Managing Documents**, shows you how to save, compare, switch between, and search a document.

In Chapter 3, **Edit Text**, you learn how to insert, edit, delete, move, and translate text as well as how to view it in various views and magnifications.

In Chapter 4, **Proofreading**, you find out how to find and replace text, correct mistakes, track changes, and more.

Chapter 5, **Format Text**, shows you how to change fonts, and text size, color, and case. You also discover the finer points of formatting text.

Chapter 6, **Format Paragraphs**, covers text alignment, line spacing, bulleted and numbered lists, tabs, indented paragraphs, and how to work with styles.

In Chapter 7, **Format Pages**, you find out how to insert page and section breaks, number lines and pages, generate a table of contents, apply a theme, and use headers, footers, and footnotes.

Chapter 8, **Print Documents**, shows you how to print a document, labels, and envelopes and how to preview a document before you print it.

In Chapter 9, **Create Tables and Charts**, you organize text quickly by creating a table and then changing its various elements to present your information in the most accessible format.

Chapter 10, **Work with Graphics**, introduces features such as WordArt, clip art, AutoShapes, text boxes, and more. You also discover how to change the appearance of your graphics and how to create a diagram.

In Chapter 11, **Customize Word**, you discover how to display formatting information and create and customize toolbars and menus, as well as how to create and run a macro.

Chapter 12, **Work with Mass Mailing Tools**, explains how to create mass mailings of letters and labels.

In Chapter 13, **Word and the Internet**, you learn how to e-mail documents, create hyperlinks, and how to save a document as a Web page.

Chapter Organization

Each chapter consists of sections, all listed in the book's table of contents. A *section* is a set of steps that shows you how to complete a specific computer task.

Each section, usually contained on two facing pages, has an introduction, full-color screen shots, steps that walk you through the task, and a tip.

What You Need to Use This Book

To perform the tasks in this book, you need a personal computer that meets the minimum requirements for any Microsoft Office 2007 product:

- Microsoft Windows XP Service Pack (SP) 2 or later, Microsoft Windows Vista, or Microsoft Windows Server 2003 (or higher) required.

- 500 megahertz (MHz) processor or higher; 256 megabyte (MB) RAM or higher

- 2 gigabyte (GB) hard disk space necessary for install; a portion of this disk space will be freed after installation if the original download package is removed from the hard drive

- DVD drive

- Minimum 800 x 600 monitor resolution; 1024 x 768 or higher recommended

- Broadband Internet connection, 128 kilobits per second (Kbps) or greater, for download and activation of products

Windows Requirements

Word 2007 will work under any version of Windows XP or Windows Vista; it will not work on earlier versions of the Windows operating system.

Monitor Resolution Differences

The figures and steps in this book were created using Windows XP with a monitor resolution of 1024 x 768. If you have set your monitor at a different resolution, you will notice differences in the appearance of the Ribbon, and those differences may affect the steps.

Using the Mouse

This book uses the following conventions to describe the actions you perform when using the mouse:

Click

Press your left mouse button once. You generally click your mouse on something to select something on the screen.

Double-click

Press your left mouse button twice. Double-clicking something on the computer screen generally opens whatever item you have double-clicked.

Right-click

Press your right mouse button. When you right-click anything on the computer screen, the program displays a shortcut menu containing commands specific to the selected item.

Click and Drag, and Release the Mouse

Move your mouse pointer and hover it over an item on the screen. Press and hold down the left mouse button. Now, move the mouse to where you want to place the item and then release the button. You use this method to move an item from one area of the computer screen to another.

The Conventions in This Book

A number of typographic and layout styles have been used throughout *Teach Yourself VISUALLY Word 2007* to distinguish different types of information.

Bold

Bold type represents the names of commands and options that you interact with. Bold type also indicates text and numbers that you must type into a dialog box or window.

Italics

Italic words introduce a new term and are followed by a definition.

Numbered Steps

You must perform the instructions in numbered steps in order to successfully complete a task and achieve the final results.

Bulleted Text

This text gives you alternative methods, explains various options, or presents what a program will do in response to the numbered steps.

Indented Text

Indented text tells you what the program does in response to you following a numbered step. For example, if you click a certain menu command, a dialog box may appear, or a window may open. Indented text may also tell you what the final result is when you follow a set of numbered steps.

Notes

Notes give additional information. They may describe special conditions that may occur during an operation. They may warn you of a situation that you want to avoid, for example the loss of data. A note may also cross-reference a related area of the book. A cross-reference may guide you to another chapter, or another section with the current chapter.

Icons

Icons are graphical representations within the text. They show you exactly what you need to click to perform a step.

 You can easily identify the tips in any task by looking for the TIP icon. Tips offer additional information, including tips, hints, and tricks. You can use the tip information to go beyond what you have learned in the steps.

In order to get this information to you in a timely manner, this book was based on a pre-release version of Microsoft Office 2007. There may be some minor changes between the screenshots in this book and what you see on your desktop. As always, Microsoft has the final word on how programs look and function; if you have any questions or see any discrepancies, consult the online help for further information about the software.

A First Look at Word

Are you ready to get started in Word? In this first chapter, you become familiar with the Word working environment and you learn basic ways to navigate and to enter text.

You can open Microsoft Word a number of ways. This section demonstrates how to open Microsoft Word from the All Programs menu. Once Word opens, a blank document, ready for you to type text, appears.

Open Word

① Click **Start**.

② Click **All Programs**.

③ Click **Microsoft Office**.

④ Click **Microsoft Office Word 2007**.

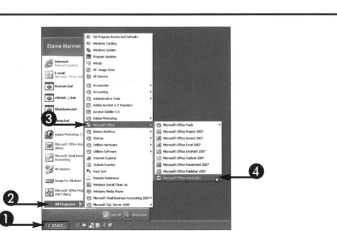

A blank document appears in the Word window.

A button representing the document appears in the Windows taskbar.

● To close Word, click the **Close** icon (✕).

The Word window contains tools you can use to work quickly and efficiently while you are creating documents.

Title Bar
Shows the program and document titles.

Office Icon
Provides access to the only menu in Word 2007. The commands on this menu start a new document, open an existing document, and save, print, and close documents.

Ribbon
Contains the commands organized in three components: tabs, groups, and commands. **Tabs** represent activities you perform in Word. They appear across the top of the ribbon and contain related groups. Some tabs, like the Table Tools tab, are context sensitive and only appear when you need them. **Groups** organize related commands; each group name appears below the group on the ribbon. **Commands** appear within each group.

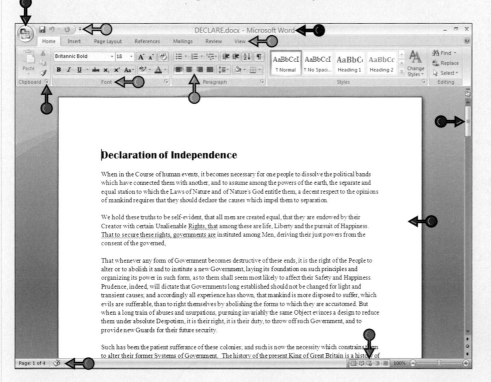

Quick Access Toolbar
Contains buttons that perform the common actions: saving a document, undoing your last action, or repeating your last action.

Status Bar
Displays document information as well as the insertion point location. From left to right, this bar contains: the number of the page on which the insertion point currently appears as well as the total number of pages in the document; the proofing errors indicator (☑); and the view buttons.

Scroll Bar
Enables you to reposition the document window vertically. Drag the scroll box within the scroll bar or click the scroll bar arrows (▲ and ▼).

Document Area
The area where you type. The flashing insertion point represents the location where text will appear when you type.

Dialog Box Launcher
The button that appears in the lower right corner of a group on the ribbon; clicking this button opens a dialog box or task pane that provides more options.

Work with the Office Button

The Office button opens the only menu in Word 2007. On this menu, you find a list of actions — commands — you can use to manage files by saving them, printing them, cleaning them up by removing sensitive information, and distributing them.

① Click the **Office** icon (🔵).

A menu opens, displaying the most commonly used file management commands.

② Click the command you want to use.

Word performs the command.

● Menus displaying side-pointing arrows display additional information to the right when you position the mouse pointer over them.

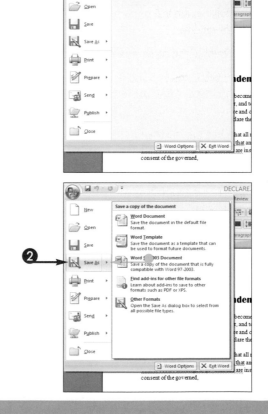

Select Commands with the Mouse

You can use the mouse to navigate the Ribbon or select a command from the Quick Access toolbar at the top of the window. The Ribbon organizes tasks using tabs. On any particular tab, you find groups of commands related to that task.

The Quick Access toolbar appears immediately beside the Office button and contains four commonly used commands: Save, Undo, Redo, and Print. Click a button to perform that command.

Select Commands with the Mouse

① Click the tab containing the command you want to use.

② Click in the text or paragraph you want to modify.

③ Point to the command you want to use.

● Word displays a ToolTip describing the function of the icon at which the mouse points.

④ Click the command.

● Word performs the command you selected.

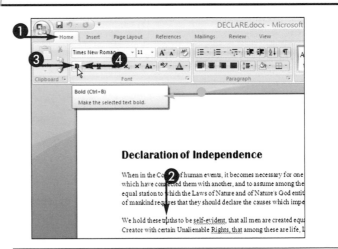

Select Commands with the Keyboard

To keep your hands on the keyboard and work efficiently, you can use your keyboard to select commands from the Ribbon or the Quick Access toolbar.

Select Commands with the Keyboard

① If appropriate for the command you intend to use, place the insertion point in the proper word or paragraph.

② Press **Alt** on the keyboard.

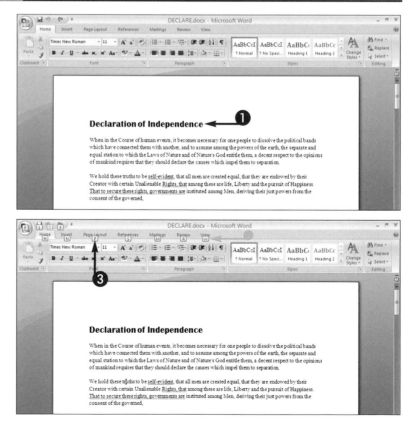

● Shortcut letters and numbers appear on the Ribbon.

Note: *The numbers control commands on the Quick Access toolbar.*

③ Press a letter to select a tab on the Ribbon.

This example presses **P**.

Note: *If you press a key you did not mean to press, press* **Esc** *to back up to your preceding action.*

● Word displays the appropriate tab and letters for each command on that tab.

④ Press a letter or letters to select a command.

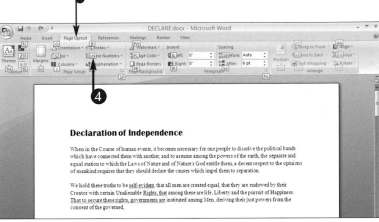

● Word displays options for the command you selected.

⑤ Press a letter or use the arrow keys on the keyboard to select an option.

Word performs the command you selected, applying the option you chose.

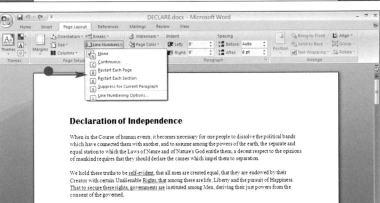

 TIPS

Is there a way to toggle between the document and the Ribbon using the keyboard?

Yes. Each time you press F6, Word changes focus of the program, switching between the document, the Status bar, and the Ribbon.

I just want to type and I do not need any commands. Can I hide the Ribbon so that I have more screen space in which to type?

Yes. Double-click any tab; Word hides the Ribbon. Double-click any tab again to redisplay the Ribbon.

Select Command Choices

In many cases, Word 2007 previews the effects of a command choice before you select it, giving you the opportunity to "try before you buy."

You cannot preview the effects of all commands, and the type of preview available varies from command to command. In addition, Live Preview does not work with the Mini Toolbar.

Select Command Choices

VIEW A LIVE PREVIEW

① Click in the word or paragraph you want to modify.

② Click the tab containing the command you are considering performing.

③ Position the mouse pointer above the command you are considering applying.

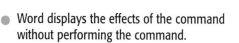

● Word displays the effects of the command without performing the command.

In this example, the paragraph containing the insertion point appears in the Heading 1 style.

On the Ribbon, the currently applied style is highlighted for the paragraph. When you position the mouse pointer over a new style, Word displays the text in the Document Area in that style and highlights the new style on the Ribbon.

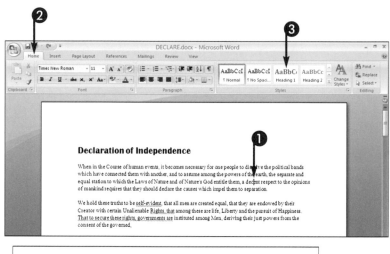

PREVIEW USING OTHER METHODS

1 Click an icon containing an arrow.

● You can view more choices.

● For some commands, you might click arrows to scroll through choices.

● You can also click the **More** icon to display a drop-down view of the choices.

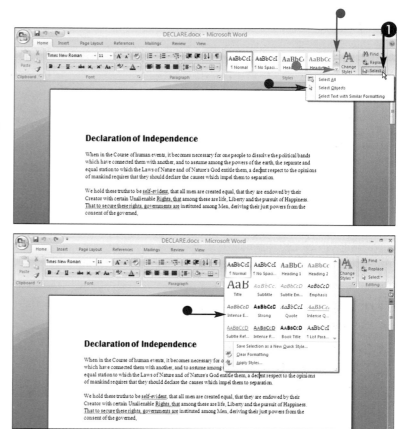

● Word displays additional choices.

2 Click a choice to select it.

Can I preview font selections?

Can I preview font selections?
Yes. Follow these steps:

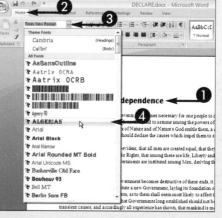

1 Click in the word or select the text you want to preview in a different font.

Note: See Chapter 3 for more on selecting text.

2 Click the **Home** tab.

3 On the Ribbon, click here to display the list of fonts.

4 Point at a font to see Word display the selected word or text in that font.

Work with the Mini Toolbar and Context Menus

You can use the Mini Toolbar and the context menu to format text without switching to the Home tab. The Mini Toolbar and the Context menu contain a combination of commands available primarily in the Font group and the Paragraph group on the Home tab.

The Mini Toolbar fades in and out when you select text.

Work with the Mini Toolbar and Context Menus

① Select text.

● The Mini Toolbar appears in the background.

② Position the mouse pointer over the Mini Toolbar to make it appear solidly.

③ Right-click the selected text.

● Both the Mini Toolbar and the context menu appear.

You can right-click anywhere, not just on selected text, to display the Mini Toolbar and the context menu.

④ Click any command or icon.

Word activates the command or icon.

Although the Ribbon contains most of the commands you use on a regular basis, you still need dialog boxes occasionally to select a command or refine a choice.

Launch a Dialog Box

1 Position the mouse pointer over a **Dialog Box launcher** icon ().

● Word displays a ToolTip that describes what will happen when you click.

2 Click .

● Word displays the dialog box.

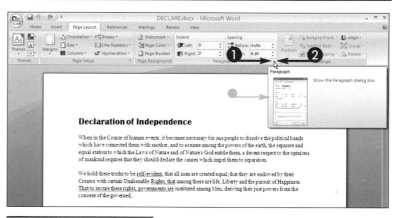

Word makes typing easy: you do not need to press Enter to start a new line. Word calculates when a new line should begin and automatically starts it for you.

When you type, you should use the Tab key instead of the spacebar to add more than one space between words. See Chapter 6 for details on setting tabs.

Enter Text

TYPE TEXT

① Type the text that you want to appear in your document.

The text appears to the left of the insertion point as you type.

As the insertion point reaches the end of the line, Word automatically starts a new one.

Press **Enter** only to start a new paragraph.

August 23, 2006

Jane Smith
Memorial Sprinklers, LLC
4816 Memorial Hwy., Suite 200
Tampa, FL 33609

Dear Ms. Smith:

Thank you for selecting Marmel Enterprises, LLC to assist you in using some of your Microsoft Office products, specifically Microsoft Office Word 2007 and Microsoft Office Excel 2007.

① → As we agreed

SEPARATE INFORMATION

① Type a word or phrase.

② Press **Tab** .

To align text properly, you press **Tab** to include more than one space between words.

Several spaces appear between the last letter you typed and the insertion point.

③ Type another word or phrase.

August 23, 2006

Jane Smith
Memorial Sprinklers, LLC
4816 Memorial Hwy., Suite 200
Tampa, FL 33609

Dear Ms. Smith:

Thank you for selecting Marmel Enterprises, LLC to assist you in using some of your Microsoft Office products, specifically Microsoft Office Word 2007 and Microsoft Office Excel 2007.

As we agreed, classes will be held as follows:

① → Class 1
→ Class 2   September 1 **③**

ENTER TEXT AUTOMATICALLY

1 Begin typing a common word, phrase, or date.

The AutoComplete feature suggests common words and phrases based on what you type.

● Word suggests the rest of the word, phrase, or month.

August 23, 2006

Jane Smith
Memorial Sprinklers, LLC
4816 Memorial Hwy., Suite 200
Tampa, FL 33609

Dear Ms. Smith:

Thank you for selecting Marmel Enterprises, LLC to assist you in using some of your Microsoft Office products, specifically Microsoft Office Word 2007 and Microsoft Office Excel 2007.

As we agreed, classes will be held as follows:

Class 1   September 1, 2006
Class 2   **1** September (Press ENTER to Insert)
Class 3   Sept

● You can press **Enter** to let Word finish typing the word, phrase, or month for you.

You can keep typing to ignore Word's suggestion.

August 23, 2006

Jane Smith
Memorial Sprinklers, LLC
4816 Memorial Hwy., Suite 200
Tampa, FL 33609

Dear Ms. Smith:

Thank you for selecting Marmel Enterprises, LLC to assist you in using some of your Microsoft Office products, specifically Microsoft Office Word 2007 and Microsoft Office Excel 2007.

As we agreed, classes will be held as follows:

Class 1   September 1, 2006
Class 2   September 10, 2006
Class 3   September

TIP

Why should I use Tab instead of Spacebar to include more than one space between words?

Typically, when you include more than one space between words or phrases, you intend to align text in a columnar fashion. Most fonts are proportional, meaning each character of a font takes up a different amount of space on a line. Therefore, you cannot calculate the number of spaces needed to align words beneath each other. Tabs, however, are set at specific locations on a line, such as 3 inches. When you press Tab, you know exactly where words or phrases appear on a line. Word sets default tabs every .5 inches; to avoid pressing Tab multiple times to separate text, change the tab settings.

Move Around in a Document

You can use many different techniques to move to a different location in a document; the technique you select depends on the location to which you want to move.

Move Around in a Document

MOVE ONE CHARACTER

1 Note the location of the insertion point.

2 Press ➡.

Declaration of **Independence**

When in the Course of human events, it becomes necessary for one people to dissolve the political bands which have connected them with another, and to assume among the powers of the earth, the separate and equal station to which the Laws of Nature and of Nature's God entitle them, a decent respect to the opinions of mankind requires that they should declare the causes which impel them to separation.

We hold these truths to be self-evident: that all men are created equal, that they are endowed by their Creator with certain Unalienable Rights, that among these are life, Liberty and the pursuit of Happiness. That to secure these rights, governments are instituted among Men, deriving their just powers from the consent of the governed.

● Word moves the insertion point one character to the right.

You can press ⬅, ⬆, or ⬇ to move the insertion point one character left, up, or down.

Holding any arrow key moves the insertion point repeatedly in the direction of the arrow key.

You can press Ctrl + ➡ or Ctrl + ⬅ to move the insertion point one word at a time to the right or left.

Declaration of **Independence**

When in the Course of human events, it becomes necessary for one people to dissolve the political bands which have connected them with another, and to assume among the powers of the earth, the separate and equal station to which the Laws of Nature and of Nature's God entitle them, a decent respect to the opinions of mankind requires that they should declare the causes which impel them to separation.

We hold these truths to be self-evident: that all men are created equal, that they are endowed by their Creator with certain Unalienable Rights, that among these are life, Liberty and the pursuit of Happiness. That to secure these rights, governments are instituted among Men, deriving their just powers from the consent of the governed.

MOVE ONE SCREEN

1 Note the last visible line on-screen.

2 Press **Page down**.

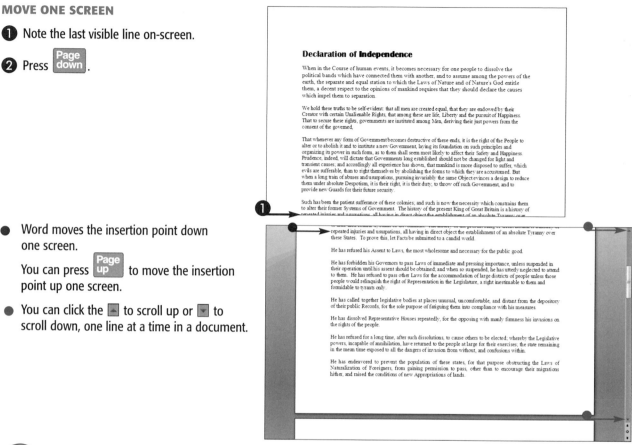

● Word moves the insertion point down one screen.

You can press **Page up** to move the insertion point up one screen.

● You can click the ▲ to scroll up or ▼ to scroll down, one line at a time in a document.

TIPS

How do I quickly move the insertion point to the beginning or the end of a document?

Press **Ctrl** + **Home** to move the insertion point to the beginning of a document or **Ctrl** + **End** to move the insertion point to the bottom of a document. You can press **Shift** + **F5** to move the insertion point to the last place you changed in your document.

Is there a way to move the insertion point to a specific location?

Yes, you can use bookmarks to mark a particular place and then return to it. See Chapter 3 for details on creating a bookmark and returning to the bookmark's location. See Chapter 4 for details on searching for a specific word and, if necessary, replacing that word with a different one.

Get Help

You can search for help with the
Word tasks you perform. By default,
Word searches the Help file on your
computer as well as the Internet.

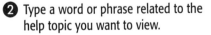

① Click the Help icon (●).

The Word Help window appears.

② Type a word or phrase related to the help topic you want to view.

③ Press Enter.

● Help topics related to the word or phrase you typed appear in the task pane.

④ Click the topic most closely related to the subject on which you want help.

● The help topic information appears in the Word Help window.

⑤ To close the Help window, click ☒.

The Word window reappears.

TIPS

Can I leave the Word Help window open while I work in Word?

Yes. Simply do not perform Step **5**. By default, the Word Help window remains on top of the Word window. You can move the Word Help window by dragging its title bar. You can resize the window by positioning the mouse pointer over any edge of the window; when the mouse pointer changes to a two-headed arrow, drag in to make the window smaller and out to make the window larger.

I want to keep the Help window open, but not in front of the Word window. Is there a way to make it drop down to the Windows Task Bar?

Yes. Click the **pushpin** icon (🖈). When you subsequently click in Word window, Word Help drops down to the Windows Task Bar. You can redisplay Word Help by clicking its task bar button.

Managing Documents

Now that you know the basics, it is time to discover how to efficiently navigate among Word documents. In this chapter, you learn how to manage the Word documents you create.

Hi Jan,
Can you send me a copy of the quarterly sales report for your division? Accounting will probably need it by end of day tomorrow.
Thanks!
Jim

FINAL

Save a
Document

You can save a document so that you can use it at another time in Microsoft Word. Word 2007 uses a new, XML-based file format that reduces the size of a Word document, improving the likelihood of recovering information from a corrupt file.

After you save a document for the first time, you can click the Save icon on the Quick Access toolbar to save it again.

① Click 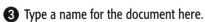.

② Click **Save As**.

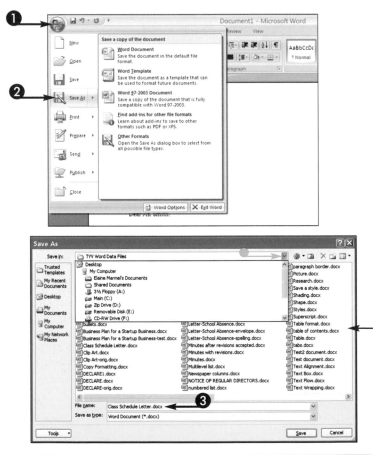

The Save As dialog box appears.

③ Type a name for the document here.

● You can click here to select a location on your computer in which to save the document.

● The files and folders stored in the folder shown in the Save in list appear here.

- You can click any of these buttons to navigate quickly to common locations to save documents.

- You can click the **Folder** icon (📁) to create a new folder in which to store the document.

- You can click the **Views** icon (▦▾) to change the view of files and folders.

④ Click **Save**.

- Word saves the document and displays the name you supplied in the title bar.

TIPS

Will my associate, who uses Word 2003, be able to open a document I save in Word 2007?

Microsoft plans to make a converter available that will enable Word 2003 users to open Word 2007 documents. To make it easier for your associate, however, you can create the document in Word 2007 but save it in Word 2003 format. See the next section, "Save a Document to Word 97-2003 Format," for more information.

How can I tell if I am working on a document saved in Word 2007 as opposed to one saved in Word 2003?

Word 2007 uses the file name extension .docx to designate its new file format, while the file name extension for a Word 2003 document is .doc. If you set your computer's folder options to display extensions of known file types, the full file name of the document appears in the title bar of the program. If you do not display extensions for known file types, you can tell you are working with a document created in Word 2003 because, in the program title bar, the file name appears, followed by Compatibility Mode in parentheses.

Save a Document to Word 97-2003 Format

You can save documents you create in Microsoft Word in a variety of other formats, such as Word templates, Microsoft Works files, text files, or Word 97-2003 format to share them with people who do not use Microsoft Word 2007.

Although the steps in this section focus on saving a document to Word 97-2003 format, you can use these steps to save a document to any file format Word supports.

① Click ▣.

② Point to **Save As**.

③ Click **Word 97-2003 Format**.

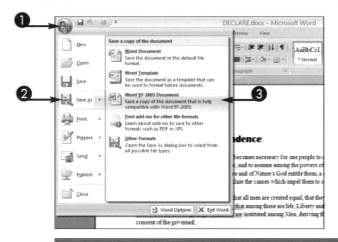

The Save As dialog box appears.

④ Type a name for the document.

● The default file type is Word 97-2003 Document (*.doc).

● You can click here to display the formats available for the document and select a different format.

⑤ Click **Save**.

Word saves the document in the format that you select.

You can save Word documents in PDF or XPS formats. Anyone using Adobe's free Acrobat Reader can open a PDF file. XPS is Microsoft's new alternative to a PDF file. Windows Vista will come with an XPS viewer and an XPS printer driver so that users of Windows Vista will be able to exchange XPS documents. To save a PDF or XPS document, you must install the Publish as PDF or XPS add-in; click Find add-ins for other file formats on the Save As menu and follow the on-screen instructions.

Choose a save option ...

Save a Document in PDF or XPS Format

1 Click .

2 Point to **Save As**.

3 Click **PDF or XPS**.

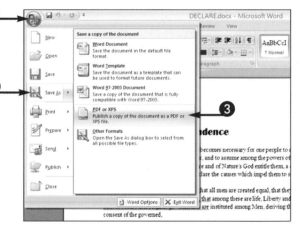

The Publish As PDF or XPS dialog box appears.

4 Type a name for the document.

● The default file type is PDF (*.pdf).

● You can click here to display the formats available for the document and select a different format.

5 Click **Publish**.

Word saves the document in the format that you select.

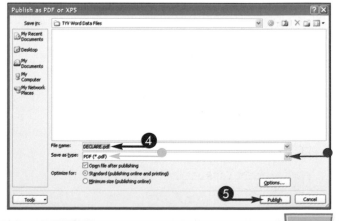

Set Options for Saving Documents

You can set a variety of options for saving documents, like whether Word creates a backup copy of your document and the location Word suggests when you save your documents.

Choose a save option ...

Option 1
Option 3
Option 2

Set Options for Saving Documents

SET FILE SAVING OPTIONS

1 Click 🔘.

2 Click **Word Options**.

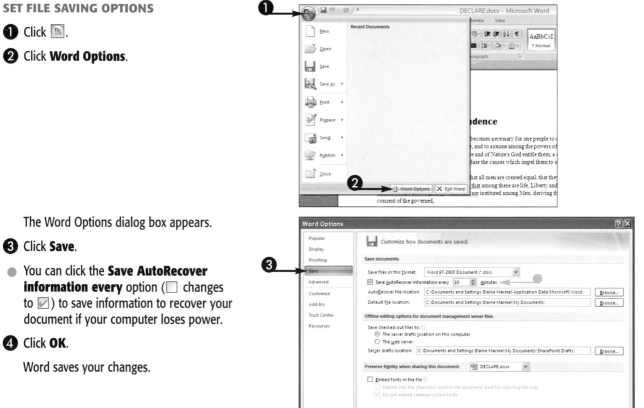

The Word Options dialog box appears.

3 Click **Save**.

● You can click the **Save AutoRecover information every** option (☐ changes to ☑) to save information to recover your document if your computer loses power.

4 Click **OK**.

Word saves your changes.

SET FILE SAVING LOCATIONS

1. Complete Steps **1** to **3** in the subsection "Set File Saving Options" on the previous page.

2. Click **Browse** next to Default file location.

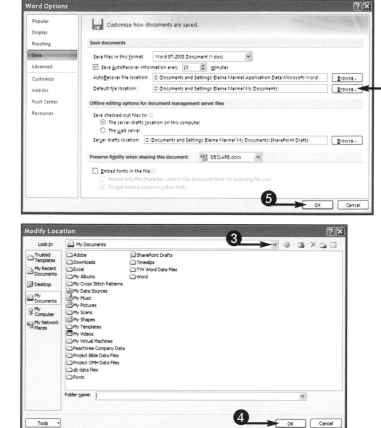

The Modify Location dialog box appears.

3. Click here to navigate to the folder where you want to save Word documents.

4. Click **OK** to redisplay the Word Options dialog box.

You can repeat Steps **3** to **4** to set the AutoRecover File and the Server drafts locations.

5. Click **OK**.

Word saves your changes.

TIP

Can I make Word automatically save a backup copy of my document?

Yes.

1. Complete Steps **1** to **2** in the subsection "Set File Saving Options" on the previous page.

2. Click **Advanced** and scroll down to the Save section.

3. Click **Always create backup copy** (☐ changes to ☑).

4. Click **OK**.

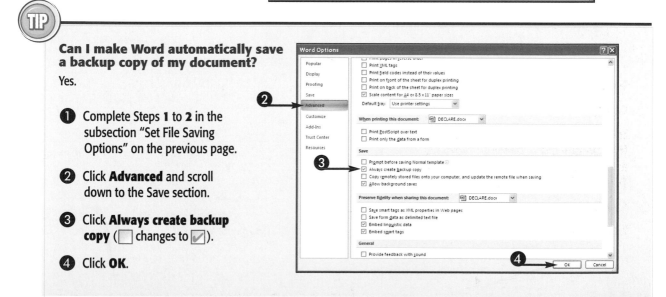

Open
Documents

You can display documents you previously saved on-screen. When you open a document, you can make changes to it.

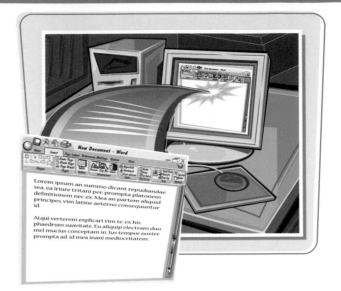

OPEN A WORD DOCUMENT

1 Click .

2 Click **Open**.

The Open dialog box appears.

3 Click here to navigate to the folder containing the document you want to open.

● You can double-click a folder to see the documents in it.

● You can click these buttons to navigate to common file locations.

④ Click the document you want to open.

⑤ Click **Open**.

The document appears on-screen.

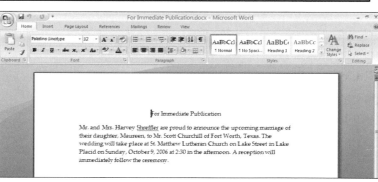

TIP

Are there other ways to open a document?

Yes. Recently opened documents appear on the Office menu, and you can click any of these documents to open them.

① Click the **Office** icon (⌐⌐).

② Click a document to open it.

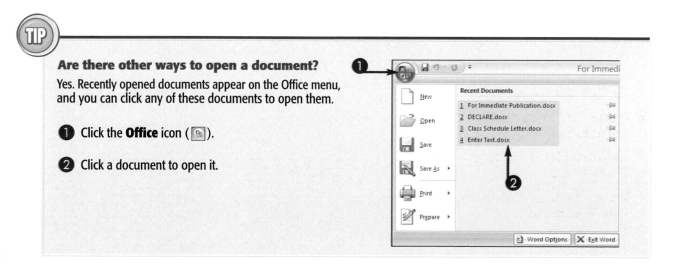

You can open documents created by colleagues using several other word processing programs besides Word.

OPEN A DOCUMENT IN ANOTHER FORMAT

1 Click 🔘.

2 Click **Open**.

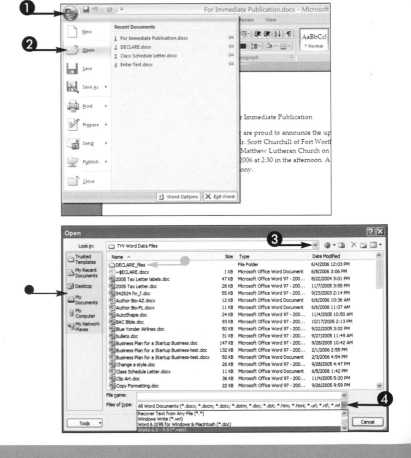

The Open dialog box appears.

3 Click here to navigate to the file you want to open.

● You can double-click a folder to view the documents in it.

● You can click these buttons to navigate to common file locations.

4 Click here to select the type of document you want to open.

⑤ Click the file you want to open.

⑥ Click **Open**.

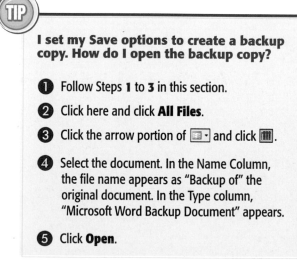

Note: *You may be prompted to install a converter to open the file; click* **Yes** *or* **OK** *to install the converter and open the file.*

● Word opens the file in Compatibility Mode.

TIP

I set my Save options to create a backup copy. How do I open the backup copy?

① Follow Steps **1** to **3** in this section.

② Click here and click **All Files**.

③ Click the arrow portion of 🔲 and click 🔳.

④ Select the document. In the Name Column, the file name appears as "Backup of" the original document. In the Type column, "Microsoft Word Backup Document" appears.

⑤ Click **Open**.

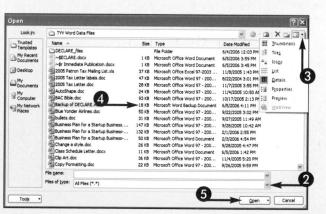

Start a New Document

Although a new, blank document appears when Word opens, you do not need to close and reopen Word to start a new, blank document.

You can use a variety of templates – documents containing predefined settings that save you the effort of creating the settings yourself – as the foundation for your documents.

① Click .

② Click **New**.

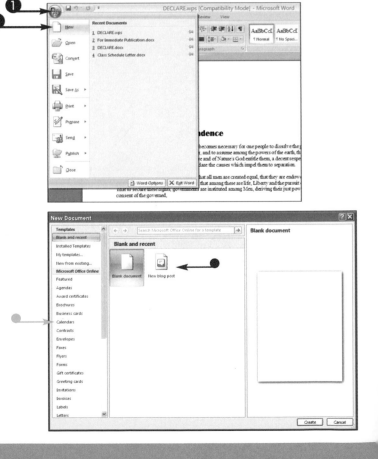

The New Document dialog box appears, displaying the most common choices.

● You can click any option in the Templates list to view sample templates on which to base a document.

● Samples of preformatted documents appear in this area.

Note: *Clicking some of the options in the Templates list displays subcategories you can click.*

③ Click in the Templates List.

④ Click a template.

⑤ Click **Create**.

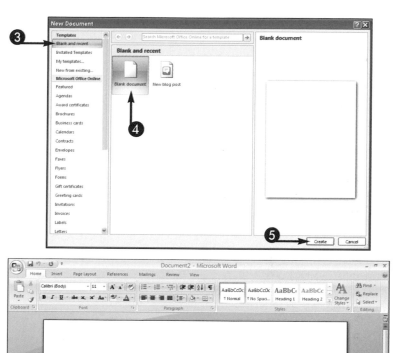

A new document appears on-screen.

You can edit this document any way you choose.

What is a template?

A template provides a foundation for a Word document. All documents are built on some template; blank documents are built on the Normal template. Using templates, your company can create documents with consistent appearances because templates contain a specific set of fonts and styles and use the same formatting. Some Word templates, like the FAX cover sheets or the forms, also contain text that helps you quickly and easily create a document. Many of the available templates come from the Office Online Web site; when you select one, you download it.

Switch Between Open Documents

If you have two or more documents open, you can switch between them from within Word or using the Windows taskbar.

If buttons representing each open document do not appear on the Windows Taskbar, you can set options to display them.

SWITCH DOCUMENTS USING WORD

① Click the **View** tab.

② Click **Switch Windows**.

● A list of all open documents appears at the bottom of the menu.

③ Click the document you want to view.

The selected document appears.

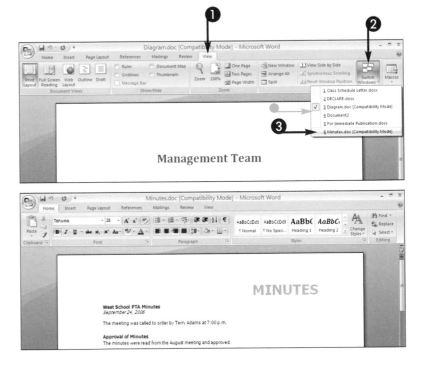

SWITCH DOCUMENTS USING THE WINDOWS TASKBAR

1 Open all the documents you want to work with.

Note: To open a document, see the section "Open Documents."

● Each open Word document appears as a button in the Windows taskbar.

2 Click the button of the document you want to view.

The document appears on-screen.

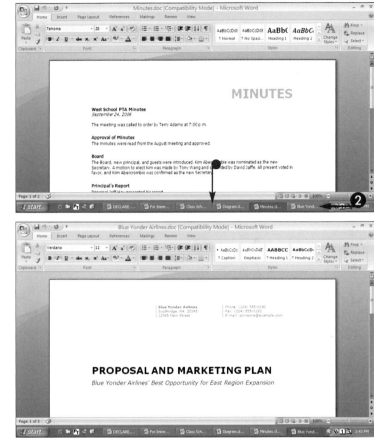

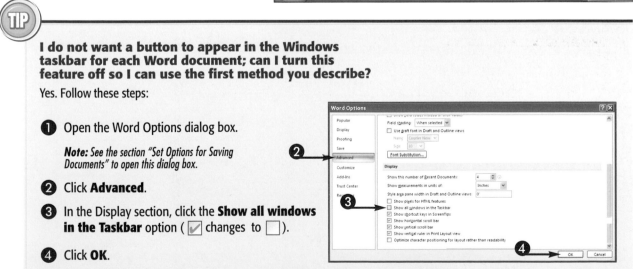

TIP

I do not want a button to appear in the Windows taskbar for each Word document; can I turn this feature off so I can use the first method you describe?

Yes. Follow these steps:

1 Open the Word Options dialog box.

Note: See the section "Set Options for Saving Documents" to open this dialog box.

2 Click **Advanced**.

3 In the Display section, click the **Show all windows in the Taskbar** option (☑ changes to ☐).

4 Click **OK**.

Compare Open Documents

You can view two open documents side by side on-screen to compare their similarities and differences.

Using the technique described in this section, you can scroll through both documents simultaneously.

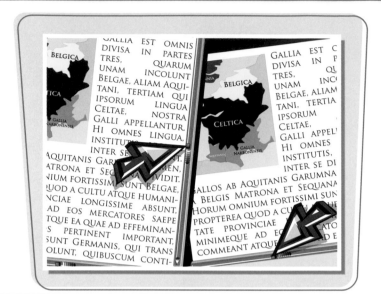

COMPARE DOCUMENTS

1 Open the two documents you want to compare.

Note: See the section "Open Documents" for details on opening a document.

2 Click the **View** tab.

3 Click **View Side by Side**.

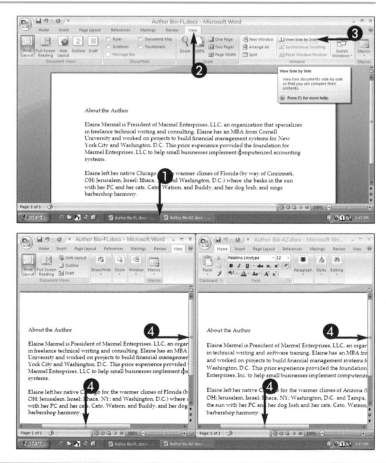

Word displays the documents in two panes beside each other.

4 Drag either document's scroll bar.

Word scrolls both documents simultaneously.

STOP COMPARING DOCUMENTS

⑤ Click **Window** in the document on the left.

Options drop down from the Window button.

⑥ Click **View Side by Side**.

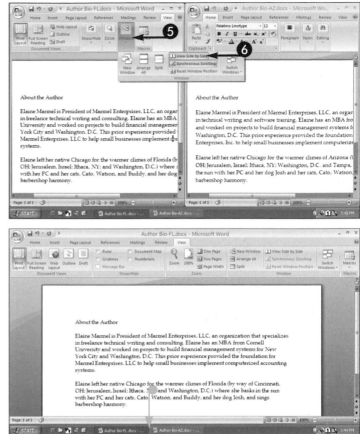

Word redisplays the document in a full screen.

The second document is still open and you can see buttons for both documents in the Windows Taskbar.

● You can switch to the other document.

Note: *For more on this technique, see the section "Switch Between Open Documents" earlier in this chapter.*

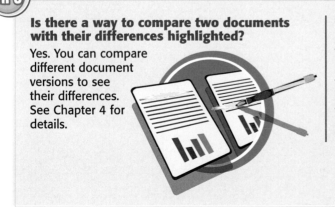

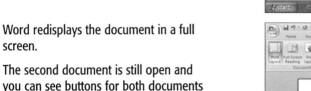

TIPS

Is there a way to compare two documents with their differences highlighted?

Yes. You can compare different document versions to see their differences. See Chapter 4 for details.

What does the Reset Window Position button do?

You can use **Arrange All** to place one window above the other, each in its own separate pane. To return to side by side viewing, click **Reset Window Position**.

Work with Document Properties

You can supply information about a document that you can then use when you search for documents.

Windows XP users can search for files using document properties by downloading Windows Desktop Search from the Microsoft Web site. Windows Vista users can use Vista's built-in search engine.

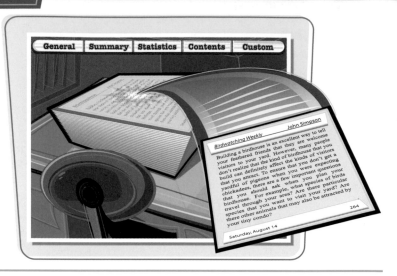

① Click 🔘.

② Point to **Prepare**.

③ Click **Properties**.

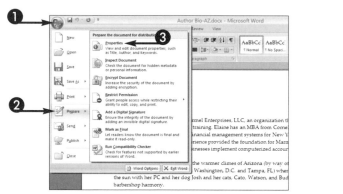

● The Document Information panel appears.

④ Type information about the document in these boxes.

⑤ Click here and select **Advanced Properties**. ④

Word displays this dialog box of additional document property information.

⑥ Change the information on the **Summary** and **Custom** tabs.

⑦ Click **OK**.

Word saves the information that you supplied.

● You can click the **Close** icon (🗙) to close the Document Information Panel.

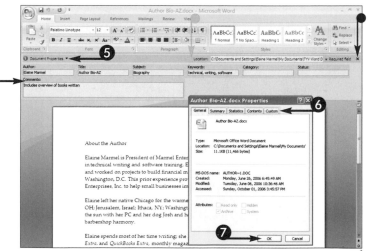

Close a Document

When you finish working with a document, you close it. If you made any changes that you did not save, Word prompts you to save them before closing the document.

---

1 Click 🔘.

2 Click **Close.**

Word removes the document from your screen.

If you had other documents open, Word displays the last document you used; otherwise, you see a blank Word window.

Inspect a Document Before Sharing

You can remove any personal information that Word stores in a document. You may want to remove this information before you share a document with anyone.

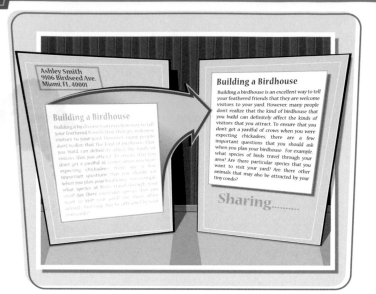

① Click 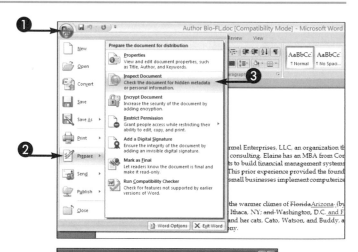.

② Point to **Prepare**.

③ Click **Inspect Document**.

*Note: If you have unsaved changes, Word prompts you to save the document, which you do by clicking **Yes**.*

The Document Inspector window appears.

● You can remove checks to avoid inspecting for these elements.

④ Click **Inspect**.

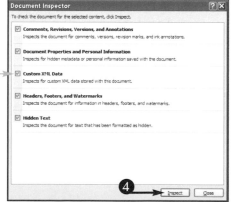

● The Document Inspector looks for the information you specified.

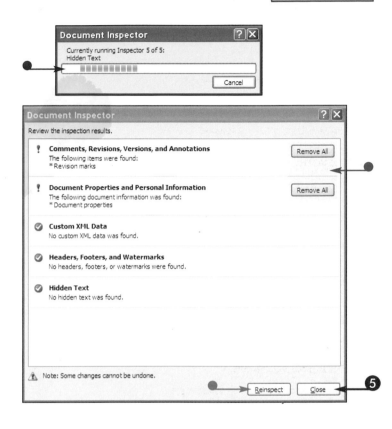

The Document Inspector displays the results.

● You can remove any identified information by clicking **Remove All** beside that element.

● You can click **Reinspect** after removing identifying information.

⑤ Click **Close**.

TIPS

Can I review the information that the Document Inspector displays before I remove it?

No. The only way to review the information before you remove it is to close the Document Inspector *without* removing information, use the appropriate Word features to review the information, and then rerun the Document Inspector as described in this section.

What happens if I remove information and then decide that I really wanted that information?

You cannot undo the effects of removing the information using the Document Inspector. However, to restore removed information, you can close the document *without* saving changes and then reopen it.

Work with Protected Documents

You can limit the changes others can make to a document by protecting it with a password.

You can limit the styles available to format the document, the kinds of changes users can make, and the users who can make changes.

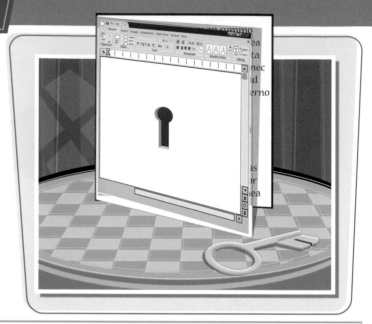

① Click the **Review** tab.

② Click **Protect Document**.

③ Click **Restrict Formatting and Editing**.

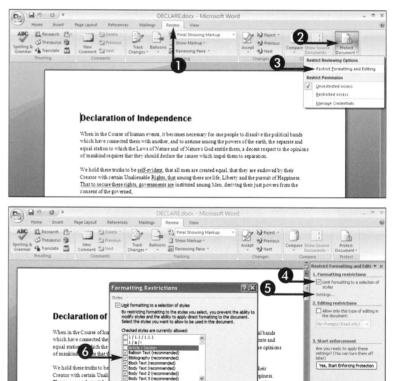

The Protect Document pane appears.

④ Click here to limit document formatting to the styles you select (☐ changes to ☑).

⑤ Click the **Settings** link.

The Formatting Restrictions dialog box appears.

⑥ Click the styles you want available (☐ changes to ☑).

⑦ Click **OK**.

8 Click here to specify editing restrictions
(☐ changes to ☑).

9 Click here and select the type of editing
to permit.

You can select parts of the document to
make them available for editing.

10 Click here to identify users allowed to
edit the selected parts of the document
(☐ changes to ☑).

11 Click **Yes, Start Enforcing Protection**.

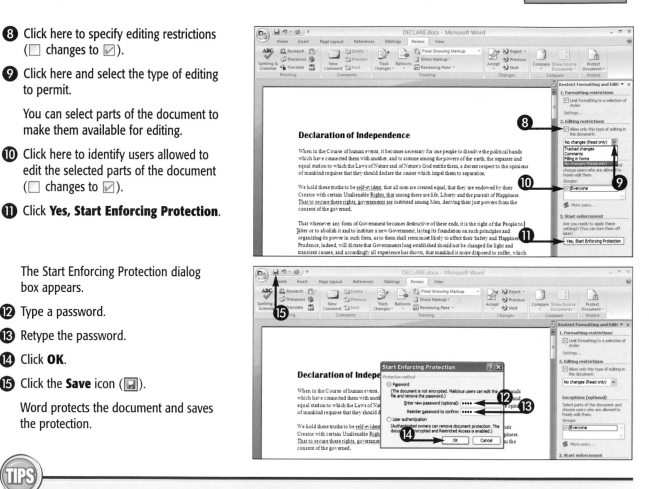

The Start Enforcing Protection dialog
box appears.

12 Type a password.

13 Retype the password.

14 Click **OK**.

15 Click the **Save** icon (🖫).

Word protects the document and saves
the protection.

TIPS

How do I open a protected document and work in it.

Open a protected document like you open any other
document. Areas you can edit are highlighted. If you
try to change an area that is not highlighted, a message
appears in the status bar, explaining that you cannot
make the modification because
that area of the document is
protected. Follow Steps **1** to
2 in this section to display
the Protect Document pane
and click **Show All Regions
I Can Edit** to find areas
you can change. To turn
off protection, you need the
protection password.

What happens when I click Restrict permission at the bottom of the Protect Document pane?

Word offers to install Windows Rights
Management, a service that helps prevent
documents and e-mail
messages from being
forwarded, edited, or
copied unless
authorized. You
can click the
**Learn more
about this feature**
link to get more
information.

Mark a Document as Final

When you mark a document as final, Word makes the document read-only; you cannot make changes to it or inspect it.

Marking a document as final is *not* a security feature; instead, it is a feature that helps you focus on *reading* rather than *editing* because it makes editing unavailable.

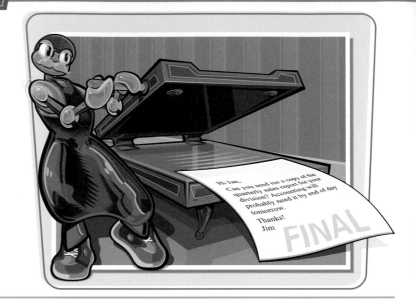

MARK THE DOCUMENT

① Click ⬛.

② Point to **Prepare**.

③ Click **Mark As Final**.

A message appears, explaining that Word will mark the document as final and then save it.

④ Click **OK**.

Word marks the document as final and then saves it, making 🖫 and other editing commands unavailable.

● The Marked as Final icon 📝 appears in the status bar.

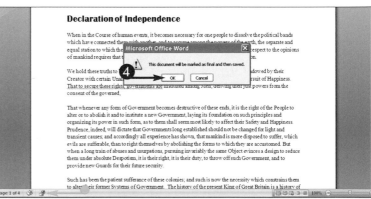

EDITING A FINAL DOCUMENT

① Click .

② Point to **Prepare**.

③ Click **Mark As Final**.

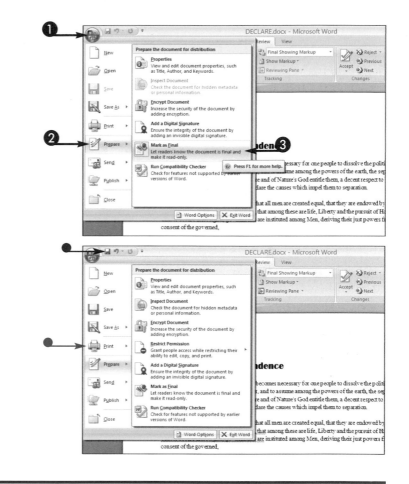

● The  becomes available.

● All options on the Office menu become available.

TIPS

Can any user remove the "Mark As Final" status from a document?

Yes. If you absolutely do not want others to edit or change your document, consider other security options. If you share a document without permitting changes, you can protect the document. You can also consider saving your document as a PDF or XPS document, all discussed earlier in this chapter.

On the Finish menu, I noticed the Add a Digital Signature command. What does this do?

You use digital signatures on documents you intend to share with others to indicate that a document has not changed since you signed it. You need a digital ID to digitally sign a document. You can purchase a digital ID or you can create your own; when you create your own digital ID, other people cannot verify the authenticity of your digital signature. Any changes to a signed document remove the signature.

Convert a Word 2003 Document to Word 2007

You can convert existing Word 97 — Word 2003 documents to the new format introduced by Word 2007.

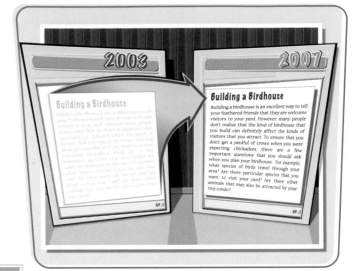

Convert a Word 2003 Document to Word 2007

1 Open any Word 2003 document.

Note: See the section "Open Documents" earlier in this chapter for details.

● In the title bar, Word 2007 indicates that the document is open in Compatibility Mode.

2 Click ⬛.

3 Click **Convert**.

Word displays a message indicating it will convert the document to the newest file format.

④ Click **OK**.

Word converts the document and removes the Compatibility Mode indicator from the title bar.

⑤ Click ▣.

The Save As dialog box appears.

● Word suggests the same file name but the new file format extension .docx

⑥ Click **Save**.

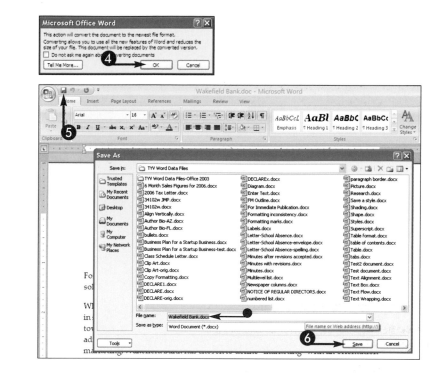

Do I need to convert my documents from earlier versions of Word before I work on them in Word 2007?

No. You can work on a document created in an older version of Word and even incorporate Word 2007 features not available in earlier versions of Word. You only need to convert documents in which you expect to include features available only in Word 2007.

Is there any difference between using the method described in this section and opening a Word 97-Word 2003 document and then using the Save As command?

Not really; using the Convert command as described in this section is simply easier because it automatically suggests the new format.

CHAPTER 3

Edit Text

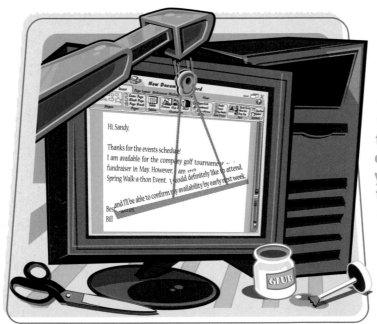

Once you know how to navigate around Word, it is time to work with the text that you type on a page. In this chapter, you learn editing techniques that you can use to change text in documents you create.

Insert Text

You can insert text into a document by adding to existing text or replacing existing text. In Overtype mode, Word replaces existing text to the right of the insertion point, character for character. In Insert mode, Word adds to existing text.

INSERT AND ADD TEXT

1 Click the location where you want to insert text.

The insertion point flashes where you clicked.

You can press →, ←, ↑, or ↓ to move the insertion point one character or line.

You can press Ctrl + → or Ctrl + ← to move the insertion point one word at a time to the right or left.

2 Type the text you want to insert.

Word inserts the text to the left of the insertion point, moving existing text to the right.

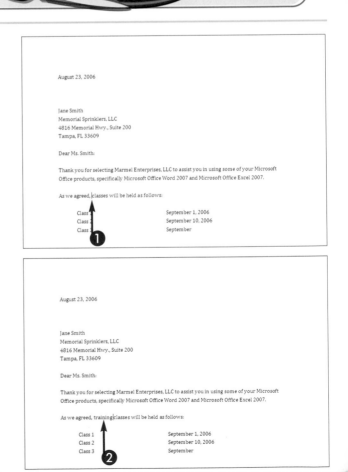

INSERT AND REPLACE TEXT

1 Right-click the status bar.

2 Click **Overtype**.

An indicator appears in the status bar.

3 Click the indicator to switch between Overtype mode and Insert mode.

4 Position the insertion point where you want to replace existing text and type the new text.

TIP

Can I control switching between Insert mode and Overtype mode using the keyboard?

Yes. Follow these steps:

1 Click the **Office** icon ( ) and click **Word Options** to display the Word Options dialog box.

2 Click **Advanced**.

3 Click **Use the Insert key to control overtype mode** (changes to).

4 Click **OK** and then press Insert on your keyboard.

Word switches between Insert mode and Overtype mode.

Delete Text

You can easily remove text from a document using either the Delete or Backspace keys on your keyboard.

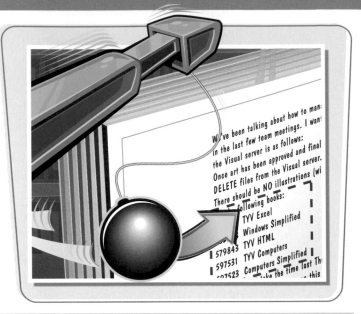

Delete Text

USING THE DELETE KEY

1 Click to the left of the location where you want to delete text.

The insertion point flashes where you clicked.

You can press ➡, ⬅, ⬆, or ⬇ to move the insertion point one character or line.

You can press `Ctrl` + ➡ or `Ctrl` + ⬅ to move the insertion point one word at a time to the right or left.

August 23, 2006

Jane Smith
Memorial Sprinklers, LLC
4816 Memorial Hwy., Suite 200
Tampa, FL 33609

Dear Ms. Smith:

Thank you for selecting Marmel Enterprises, LLC to assist you in using some of your Microsoft
Office products, specifically Microsoft Office Word 2007 and Microsoft Office Excel 2007.

As we agreed, classes will be held as follows:

Class 1	September 1, 2006
Class 2	September 10, 2006
Class 3	September

2 Press `Delete` on your keyboard.

● Word deletes the character immediately to the right of the insertion point.

You can hold `Delete` to repeatedly delete characters to the right of the insertion point.

You can press `Ctrl` + `Delete` to delete the word to the right of the insertion point.

August 23, 2006

Jane Smith
Memorial Sprinklers, LLC
4816 Memorial Hwy., Suite 200
Tampa, FL 33609

Dear Ms. Smith:

Thank you for selecting Marmel Enterprises, LLC to assist you in using some of your Microsoft Office
products, specifically Microsoft Office Word 2007 and Microsoft Office Excel 2007.

As we agreed, classes will be held as follows:

Class 1	September 1, 2006
Class 2	September 10, 2006
Class 3	September

USING THE BACKSPACE KEY

1 Click to the right of the location where you want to delete text.

The insertion point flashes where you clicked.

2 Press **Backspace** on your keyboard.

● Word deletes the character immediately to the left of the insertion point.

You can hold **Backspace** to repeatedly delete characters to the left of the insertion point.

You can press **Ctrl** + **Backspace** to delete the word to the left of the insertion point.

TIPS

Do I have to delete a large block of text one character or one word at a time?

No. You can select the block of text and then press either **Delete** or **Backspace**; either key deletes selected text. For details on selecting text, see the section "Select Text," later in this chapter.

What should I do if I mistakenly delete text?

You should use the Undo feature in Word to restore the text you deleted. For details on how this feature works, see the section "Undo Changes," later in this chapter.

Insert Blank Lines

You can insert blank lines in your text to signify new paragraphs by inserting line breaks or paragraph marks. You use line breaks to start a new line without starting a new paragraph.

Word stores paragraph formatting in the paragraph mark shown in this section. When you start a new paragraph, you can change the new paragraph's formatting without affecting the preceding paragraph's formatting. For more information on styles and displaying paragraph marks, see Chapter 6.

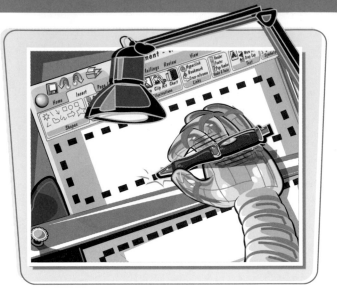

Insert Blank Lines

START A NEW PARAGRAPH

1 Press Enter.

● Word inserts a paragraph mark.

2 Repeat Step **1** for each blank line you want to insert.

INSERT A LINE BREAK

1 Press **Shift** + **Enter**.

● Word inserts a line break.

Undo Changes

You can use the Undo feature to reverse actions you take while working in a document, such as deleting or formatting text.

The Undo feature is particularly useful if you mistakenly delete text; when you use the Undo feature, you can recover the text.

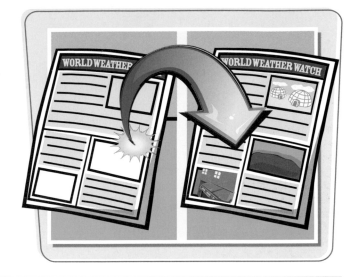

Undo Changes
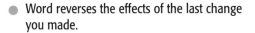

1 Click the **Undo** icon ( ).

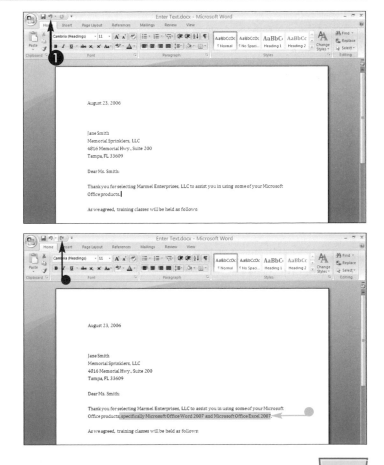

● Word reverses the effects of the last change you made.

You can repeatedly click to reverse each action you have taken, from last to first.

You can press Ctrl + Z to reverse an action.

● If you decide not to reverse an action after clicking , click the **Redo** icon ( ).

Select Text

Before performing many tasks in Word, you identify the existing text on which you want to work by selecting it. For example, you select existing text to underline it, align it, change its font size, or apply color to it.

SELECT A BLOCK OF TEXT

1. Position the mouse pointer to the left of the first character you want to select.

2. Click and drag to the right and down over the text you want to select.

   The selection appears highlighted.

   To cancel a selection, you can press →, ←, ↑, or ↓, or click anywhere on-screen.

SELECT A WORD

1. Double-click the word you want to select.

   Word selects the word.

● After releasing the mouse button, the Mini Toolbar appears faded in the background.

   You can slide the mouse pointer closer to the Mini Toolbar to make its options available.

Note: See Chapter 1 for details on using the Mini Toolbar.

August 23, 2006

Jane Smith
Memorial Sprinklers, LLC
4816 Memorial Hwy., Suite 200
Tampa, FL 33609

Dear Ms. Smith:

Thank you for selecting Marmel Enterprises, LLC to assist you in using some of your Microsoft Office products, specifically Microsoft Office Word 2007 and Microsoft Office Excel 2007.

As we agreed, classes will be held as follows:

Class 1   September 1, 2006
Class 2   September 10, 2006
Class 3   September 20, 2006

August 23, 2006

Jane Smith
Memorial Sprinklers, LLC
4816 Memorial Hwy., Suite 200
Tampa, FL 33609

Dear Ms. Smith:

Thank you for selecting Marmel Enterprises, LLC to assist you in using some of your Microsoft Office products, specifically Microsoft Office Word 2007 and Microsoft Office Excel 2007.

As we agreed, classes will be held as follows:

Class 1   September 1, 2006
Class 2   September 10, 2006
Class 3   September 20, 2006

Marmel Enterprises, LLC looks forward to helping you choose how best to use these products to

SELECT A SENTENCE

1 Press and hold `Ctrl`.

2 Click anywhere in the sentence you want to select.

Word selects the entire sentence.

● After releasing the mouse button, the Mini Toolbar appears faded in the background.

You can slide the mouse pointer closer to the Mini Toolbar to make its options available.

Note: See Chapter 1 for details on using the Mini Toolbar.

SELECT THE ENTIRE DOCUMENT

1 Click the **Home** tab.

2 Click **Select**.

3 Click **Select All**.

● Word selects the entire document.

You also can press and hold `Ctrl` and press `A` to select the entire document.

To cancel the selection, click anywhere.

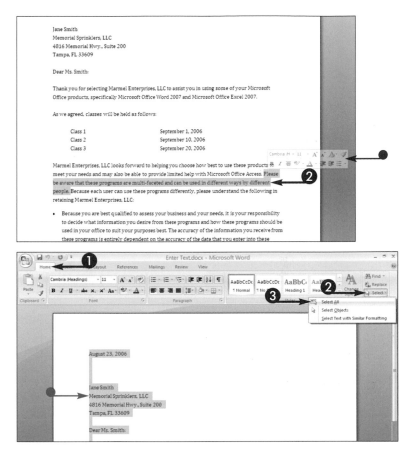

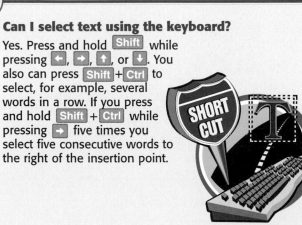

Can I select text using the keyboard?

Yes. Press and hold `Shift` while pressing `◄`, `►`, `▲`, or `▼`. You also can press `Shift` + `Ctrl` to select, for example, several words in a row. If you press and hold `Shift` + `Ctrl` while pressing `►` five times you select five consecutive words to the right of the insertion point.

Can I select noncontiguous text?

Yes. You select the first area using any of the techniques described in this section. Then, press and hold `Ctrl` as you select the additional areas. Word selects all areas, even if text appears between them.

Mark and Find Your Place

You can use the Bookmark feature to mark a location in a document so that you can easily return to it later.

You can also use bookmarks to store text; and Word uses bookmarks behind the scenes to operate some of its features.

Mark and Find Your Place

MARK YOUR PLACE

① Click the location you want to mark.

Note: If you select text instead of clicking at the location you want to mark, Word creates a bookmark containing text.

② Click the **Insert** tab.

③ Click **Bookmark**.

The Bookmark dialog box appears.

④ Type a name for the bookmark.

⑤ Click **Add**.

Word saves the bookmark and closes the Bookmark dialog box.

FIND YOUR PLACE

① Click the **Home** tab.

② Click the down arrow beside **Find**.

③ Click **Go To**.

The Go To tab of the Find and Replace dialog box appears.

④ Click **Bookmark**.

⑤ Click here and select a bookmark.

⑥ Click **Go To**.

● Word moves the insertion point to the bookmark.

● A bookmark containing text surrounds the text with brackets ([ ]).

Note: *If the bookmark contains text, Word moves the insertion point to the beginning of the bookmark.*

⑦ Press **Esc**.

Word closes the Find and Replace dialog box.

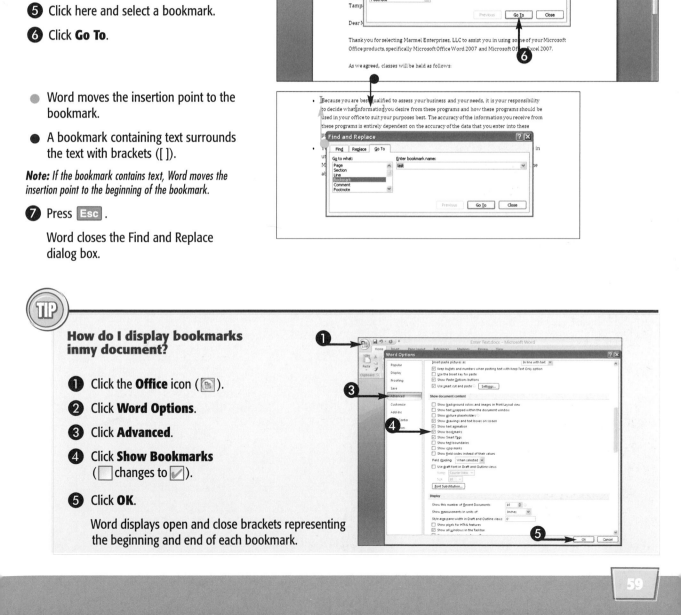

TIP

How do I display bookmarks in my document?

① Click the **Office** icon (⬚).

② Click **Word Options**.

③ Click **Advanced**.

④ Click **Show Bookmarks** (☐ changes to ☑).

⑤ Click **OK**.

Word displays open and close brackets representing the beginning and end of each bookmark.

Move or Copy Text

You can reposition text in your document by cutting and then pasting it. You also can repeat text by copying and then pasting it.

When you move text by cutting and pasting it, the text disappears from the original location and appears in a new one. When you copy and paste text, the text remains in the original location and also appears in a new one.

Move or Copy Text

USING TOOLBAR BUTTONS

1. Select the text you want to move or copy.

Note: To select text, see the section "Select Text."

2. Click the **Home** tab.

3. To move or copy text, click either the **Cut** icon (⚇) or the **Copy** icon (⚇).

4. Click to place the insertion point at the location where you want the text to appear.

5. Click the **Paste** icon (⚇).

    The text appears at the new location.

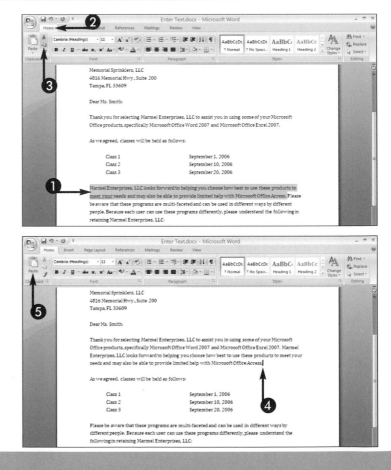

DRAGGING AND DROPPING

1 Select the text you want to move or copy.

2 Position the mouse pointer over the selected text (I changes to $\&$).

3 Either move or copy the text.

To move text, drag the mouse (I changes to $\&$).

To copy text, press and hold **Ctrl** and drag the mouse (I changes to $\&$).

● The text appears at the new location.

Dear Ms. Smith:

Thank you for selecting Marmel Enterprises, LLC to assist you in using some of your Microsoft Office products, specifically Microsoft Office Word 2007 and Microsoft Office Excel 2007. Marmel Enterprises, LLC looks forward to helping you choose how best to use these products to meet your needs and may also be able to provide limited help with Microsoft Office Access.   **1**

As we agreed, classes will be held as follows:

Class 1	September 1, 2006
Class 2	September 10, 2006
Class 3	September 20, 2006

3

Please be aware that these programs are multi-faceted and can be used in different ways by different people. Because each user can use these programs differently, please understand the following in retaining Marmel Enterprises, LLC:

- Because you are best qualified to assess your business and your needs, it is your responsibility to decide what information you desire from these programs and how these programs should be used in your office to suit your purposes best. The accuracy of the information you receive from these programs is entirely dependent on the accuracy of the data that you enter into these programs.

- Your success with these programs is contingent upon your company's interest and diligence in utilizing the system based upon the instruction and information that you will receive from

---

Dear Ms. Smith:

Thank you for selecting Marmel Enterprises, LLC to assist you in using some of your Microsoft Office products, specifically Microsoft Office Word 2007 and Microsoft Office Excel 2007. Marmel Enterprises, LLC looks forward to helping you choose how best to use these products to meet your needs and may also be able to provide limited help with Microsoft Office Access.

As we agreed, classes will be held as follows:

Class 1	September 1, 2006
Class 2	September 10, 2006
Class 3	September 20, 2006

Marmel Enterprises, LLC looks forward to helping you choose how best to use these products to meet your needs and may also be able to provide limited help with Microsoft Office Access. Please be aware that these programs are multi-faceted and can be used in different ways by different people. Because each user can use these programs differently, please understand the following in retaining Marmel Enterprises, LLC:

- Because you are best qualified to assess your business and your needs, it is your responsibility to decide what information you desire from these programs and how these programs should be used in your office to suit your purposes best. The accuracy of the information you receive from these programs is entirely dependent on the accuracy of the data that you enter into these programs.

- Your success with these programs is contingent upon your company's interest and diligence in

---

TIPS

Is there a way I can move or copy text using menus?

Yes. You can select the text that you want to move or copy and then right-click it. The context menu and the Mini Toolbar appear; click **Cut** or **Copy**. Then, place the insertion point at the location where you want the text to appear and right-click again. From the context menu, click **Paste**.

Is there a way I can move several selections at the same time?

Yes, you can use the Office Clipboard. Click the Clipboard launcher to display the Clipboard task pane, which holds up to the last 24 selections that you cut or copied. Cut each selection you want to move. Then, place the insertion point in the document where you want the text to appear. Click a selection in the Clipboard task pane to place it in the document.

Share Text Between Documents

When you cut, copy, and paste text, you are not limited to using the text in a single document. You can move or copy text from one document to another.

Any text that you cut disappears from its original location. Text that you copy continues to appear in its original location.

Share Text Between Documents

① Open the two documents you want to use to share text.

② Select the text you want to move or copy.

Note: *For details on selecting text, see the section "Select Text."*

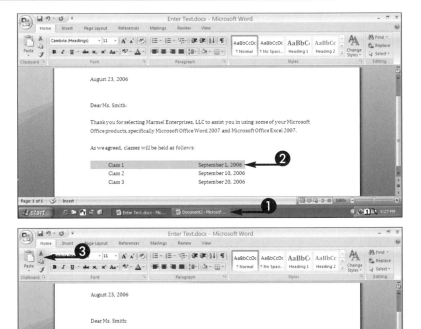

③ Click 🗴 to move text or 🗈 to copy text.

④ Switch to the other document by clicking its button in the Windows taskbar.

The other document appears.

5 Place the insertion point at the location where the text you are moving or copying should appear.

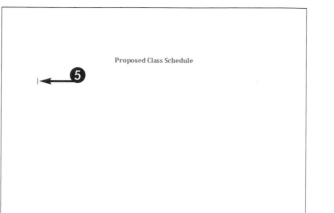

6 Click [icon].

● The text appears in the new location.

TIPS

Why do I see an icon when I paste?

Word displays the **Paste options** icon ([icon]) to give you the opportunity to determine how to handle the formatting of the selection you are pasting. Click [icon] if you want to keep the original formatting of the selection or to apply the formatting of the paragraph where the text appears after you have pasted it.

What format will Word use by default for text I paste?

The default appearance of pasted text depends on whether you included the paragraph mark, which stores paragraph formatting information, in the selection you cut or copied. If you include the paragraph mark, Word pastes the formatting stored in the paragraph mark. When you exclude the paragraph mark, Word applies character styles or formatting but does not apply paragraph styles.

Switch Document Views

You can view a document five different ways. The view you should use depends entirely on what you are doing at the time; select the view that best meets your needs. For more on the various views, see the section "Understanding Document Views."

The button for the currently selected view appears in orange.

① Click the **View** tab.

② Click one of the Document Views buttons on the Ribbon:

⬚ Print Layout

⬚ Full Screen Reading

⬚ Web Layout

⬚ Outline

⬚ Draft

Word switches your document to the view you selected.

● Icons for each view also appear at the right edge of the status bar; position the mouse pointer over each icon to see its function and click an icon to switch views.

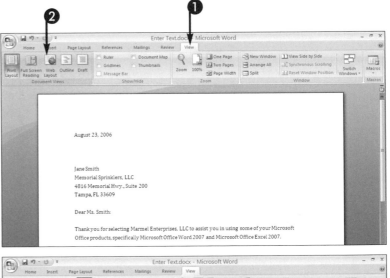

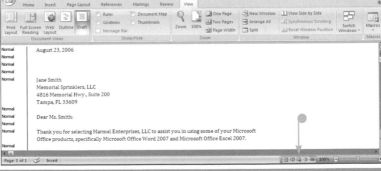

As mentioned in the section "Switch Document Views," you should select the view that best meets your needs. But, which view is right for you? The purpose of each view is described in this section.

To switch between views, see the section "Switch Document Views."

Draft View

Draft view is designed for editing and formatting; it does not display your document the way it will print. Instead, you can view elements such as the Style Area on the left side of the screen, but you cannot view the document's margins, headers and footers, or graphics in the location where they will appear.

Full Screen Reading View

Full Screen Reading view is designed to minimize eye strain when you read a document on-screen. This view removes most toolbars. To return to another view, click the **Print Layout** icon (▣) in the upper right corner of the screen.

Print Layout View

Print Layout view presents a "what you see is what you get" view of your document. In Print Layout view, you see elements of your document that affect the printed page, such as margins.

Outline View

Outline view helps you work with the organization of a document. Word indents text styled as headings based on the heading number; you can move or copy entire sections of a document by moving or copying the heading.

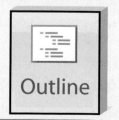

Web Layout View

Web Layout view is useful when you are designing a Web page.

You can use the Document Map view to navigate through a document that contains text styled in one of the Heading styles.

The Document Map pane is blank for documents that do not contain Heading styles. For more information on styles, see Chapter 6.

1 In a document containing text styled with Heading styles, click the **View** tab.

2 Click **Document Map**.

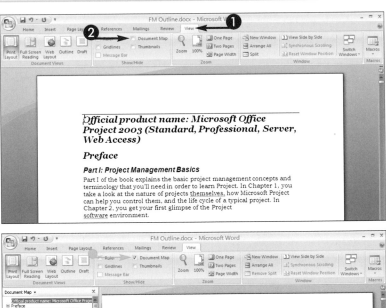

● ☐ changes to ☑ and the Document Map pane appears.

Each item in the Document Map pane represents a heading in your document; you can click any item to move the insertion point to that place in the document.

● You can click a minus sign (☐) to hide subheadings.

You can repeat Steps **1** to **2** to hide the Document Map pane.

You can view thumbnails of each page in your document to get an impression of the visual appearance of each page.

You can also navigate to various pages using thumbnails. Thumbnails are not available in Web Layout view or when you are using the Document Map.

Using Thumbnails

① Click the **View** tab.

② Click **Thumbnails**.

● ☐ changes to ☑ and Word displays thumbnail views of each page in your document.

③ Click a thumbnail to view that page.

You can repeat Steps **1** to **2** to hide the thumbnails.

Zoom In or Out

You can use the Zoom feature to enlarge or reduce the size of the text on-screen. Zooming in enlarges text. Zooming out reduces text, providing more of an overview of your document.

① Click the **View** tab.

② Click **Zoom**.

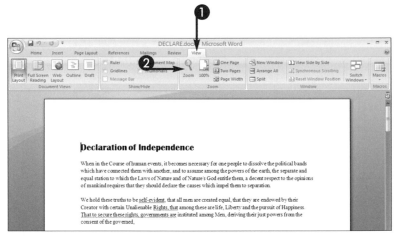

The Zoom dialog box appears.

③ Click a zoom setting.

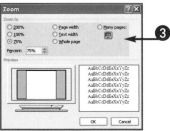

You can click the **Many pages** icon () and select to display multiple pages.

Note: The number of pages you can view depends on the resolution you set for your monitor.

4 Click **OK**.

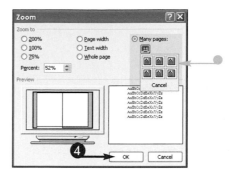

The document appears on-screen using the new zoom setting.

Zoom settings do not affect the arrangement of text when you print the document.

What do the Page width and Text width options do?

You can click **Page width** to fit the page, including margins, across the width of the screen, or **Text width** to fit text, excluding margins, across the width of the screen. The Page Width button on the Ribbon serves the same purpose as the Page width option in the Zoom dialog box, and the One Page button and the Two Pages button on the Ribbon are the most common choices when using the Many pages option in the Zoom dialog box.

Can I use the mouse to zoom?

Yes. Drag the Zoom slider in the status bar or click the plus or minus signs at either end of the Zoom slider. Each click of the plus sign zooms in 10%; each click of the minus sign zooms out 10%.

Insert a Symbol

Using the Symbol feature, you can insert characters into your documents that do not appear on your keyboard.

Insert a Symbol

1 Click the location in the document where you want the symbol to appear.

2 Click **Insert**.

3 Click **Symbol**.

A list of commonly used symbols appears.

4 Click **More Symbols**.

The Symbol dialog box appears.

5 Click here and select the symbol's font.

The available symbols change to match the font you selected.

6 Click a symbol.

7 Click **Insert**.

8 Click **Close** to close the Symbol dialog box.

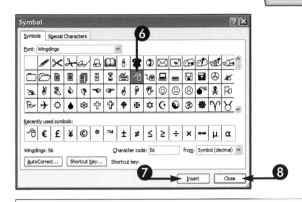

● The symbol appears in the document.

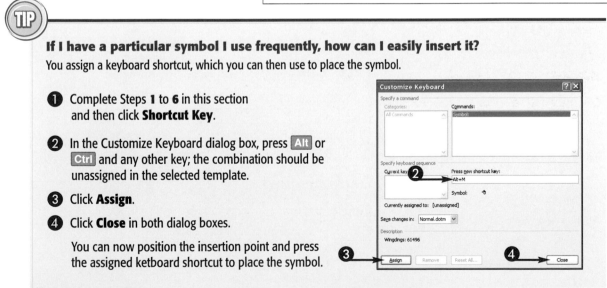

TIP

If I have a particular symbol I use frequently, how can I easily insert it?
You assign a keyboard shortcut, which you can then use to place the symbol.

1 Complete Steps **1** to **6** in this section and then click **Shortcut Key**.

2 In the Customize Keyboard dialog box, press **Alt** or **Ctrl** and any other key; the combination should be unassigned in the selected template.

3 Click **Assign**.

4 Click **Close** in both dialog boxes.

You can now position the insertion point and press the assigned ketboard shortcut to place the symbol.

Work with Equations

You can easily create complex equations in Word 2007 using the Equation Tools Design tab on the Ribbon. You no longer need to use add-in products as you did in previous versions of Word.

If you add a structure to an equation, Word supplies dotted box placeholders for you to click and substitute constants or variables. Note that Equations do not function when you work in Compatibility mode.

Work with Equations

INSERT AN EQUATION

① Position the insertion point where you want to insert an equation.

② Click **Insert**.

③ Click ▼ on the **Equation** button.

● The Equation Gallery, a list of commonly used equations, appears.

You can click an equation to insert it.

④ Click **Insert New Equation**.

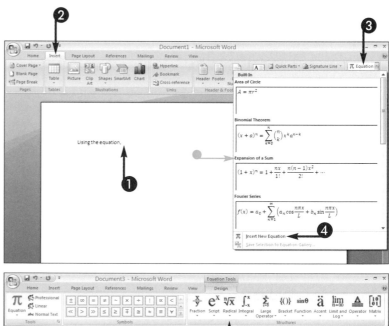

● Word inserts a blank equation box and displays the Equations Tools Design tab on the Ribbon.

⑤ Type your equation.

You can click the tools on the Ribbon to help you type the equation.

⑥ Press ➡ or click outside the equation box.

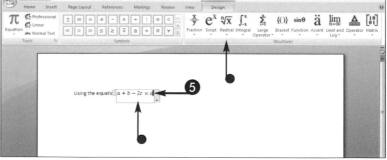

Word hides the equation box and you can continue typing.

Using the equation $a + b - 2c = d$ you can calculate

DELETE AN EQUATION

① Click in the equation to display the equation box.

② Click the three dots on the left side of the box.

Word highlights the contents of the equation box.

③ Press **Delete**.

Word deletes the equation from your document.

Using the equation $a + b - \frac{1}{2} = d$

TIP

Can I save an equation I use regularly so that I do not have to create it each time I need it?

Yes. Follow these steps:

① Click in the equation.

② Click the three dots on the left side of the box.

③ Click **Equation**.

④ Click **Save Selection to Equation Gallery**.

In the Create New Building Block dialog box that appears, click **OK**.

The next time you display the Equation Gallery, your equation appears on the list.

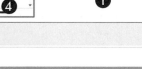

Using Smart Tags

You can use Smart Tags to save time. Using Smart Tags, Word can convert measurements, open another program to get driving directions or a map to a location, or schedule a meeting.

Word recognizes certain types of text and identifies them as smart tags by displaying a dotted purple line beneath them. By default, Word recognizes measurements.

Using Smart Tags

① Position the mouse pointer over a smart tag.

● The **Smart Tag Actions** icon () appears.

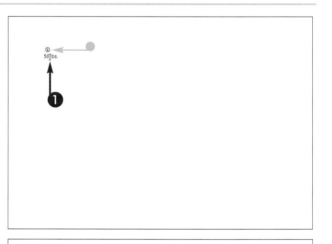

② Click .

This displays a list of actions you can take using the smart tag.

③ Click an action.

Word performs the action; or, the program that performs the action you selected appears on-screen.

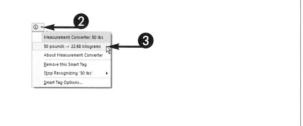

You can control the kinds of information Word recognizes and identifies as smart tags.

You also can turn off smart tag recognition entirely.

Set Smart Tag Options

1 Click 🔘.

2 Click **Word Options**.

The Word Options dialog box appears.

3 Click **Proofing**.

4 Click **AutoCorrect Options**.

The AutoCorrect dialog box appears.

5 Click the **Smart Tags** tab.

● You can click here (☑ changes to ☐) to turn off smart tag recognition.

6 Click the check box beside an item to turn smart tag recognition on (☑) or off (☐).

7 Click **OK** twice.

Word saves your preferences.

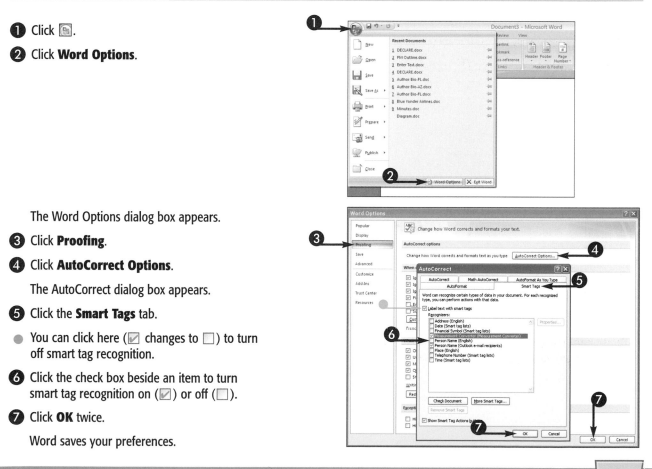

Translate Text

Using the Translation feature, you can translate a word from one language to another using language dictionaries installed on your computer.

If you are connected to the Internet, the Translation feature searches the dictionaries on your computer as well as online dictionaries.

① Select the word you want to translate.

② Click the **Review** tab.

③ Click **Translate**.

The Research task pane appears.

● The word you selected appears here.

● The current language translation pair appears here.

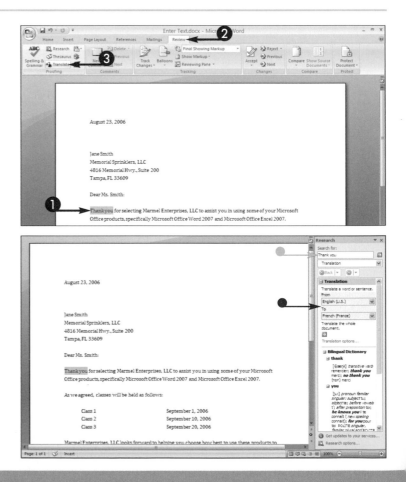

④ Click here to display the languages available into which you can translate the selected word.

⑤ Click a language.

● The translation appears here.

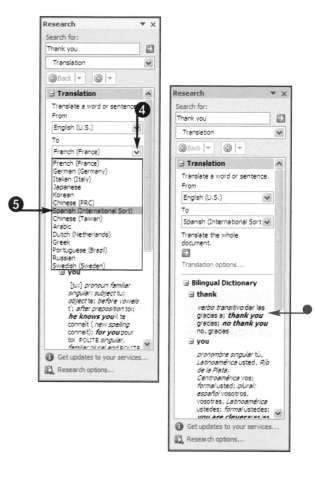

No results were found when I tried to translate a word; what should I do?

Scroll down in the Research pane. You will find that Word suggests a variety of alternative spellings for the word you tried to translate. If none of them is correct, scroll further; you can try searching **All Reference Books** and **All Research Sites** by clicking their links.

Can the Translation feature translate my entire document?

Yes and no. While the feature is capable of fairly complex translations, it may not grasp the tone or meaning of your text. You can send the document over the Internet for translation, but be aware that Word sends documents as unencrypted HTML files. If security is an issue, do not choose this route; instead, consider hiring a professional translator.

CHAPTER

4

Proofreading

This chapter shows you how to handle proofreading tasks in Word.

Search for Text

Occasionally, you need to search for a word or phrase in a document. You may also need to change that word or phrase. Using Find and Replace, you can search and substitute as needed.

Search for Text

① Click the **Home** tab.

② Click **Find**.

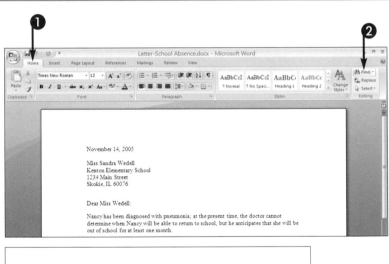

The Find and Replace window appears.

③ Type the word or phrase you want to search for.

④ Click **Find Next**.

● You can click **Reading Highlight** and then click **Highlight All** to have Word highlight each occurrence of the word in yellow.

To clear yellow highlighting, you can click **Reading Highlight** and click **Clear Highlighting**.

● You can click **Find in** to limit the search to the main document or the headers and footers.

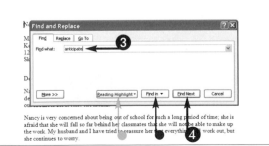

● Word highlights the first occurrence of the word or phrase.

● You can click **Find Next** again to find additional occurrences of the word or phrase.

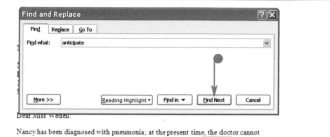

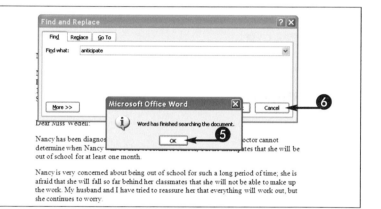

When Word finds no more occurrences of the word or phrase, a dialog box appears telling you that the search is finished.

5 Click **OK**.

The Cancel button in the Find and Replace window changes to Close.

6 Click **Close** to close the Find and Replace window.

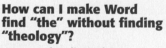

TIPS

Does the location of the insertion point matter when I start searching?

Not really. Word searches from the location of the insertion point down through the end of the document and then, if necessary, continues searching from the beginning of the document. The search ends when Word reaches the location of the insertion point where the search began.

How can I make Word find "the" without finding "theology"?

You need to limit the search to whole words only. In the Find and Replace window, click **More**; the button name changes to Less, and the window expands to show additional options. Click the check box beside **Find whole words only** (☐ changes to ☑).

Substitute Text

Often, you want to find a word or phrase because you need to substitute some other word or phrase for it.

You can substitute a word or phrase for all occurrences of the original word or phrase, or you can selectively substitute.

Substitute Text

1 Click the **Home** tab.

2 Click **Replace**.

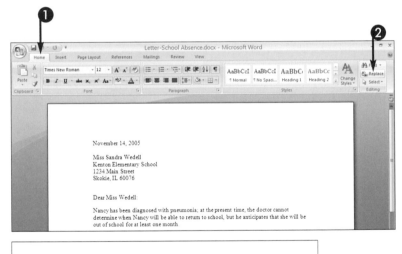

The Find and Replace window appears.

3 Type the word or phrase you want to replace here.

4 Type the word or phrase you want Word to substitute here.

5 Click **Find Next**.

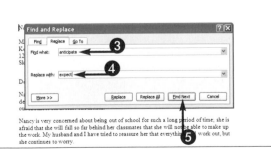

- Word highlights the first occurrence of the word or phrase that it finds.

- If you do not want to change the highlighted occurrence, you can click **Find Next** to ignore it.

6 Click **Replace**.

- To change all occurrences, you can click **Replace All**.

  Word replaces the original word or phrase with the word or phrase you specify as the substitute.

7 Repeat Steps **5** to **6**, replacing or ignoring words or phrases as appropriate.

  When Word finds no more occurrences of the word or phrase, a dialog box appears.

8 Click **OK**.

  The Cancel button in the Find and Replace window changes to Close.

9 Click **Close** to close the Find and Replace window.

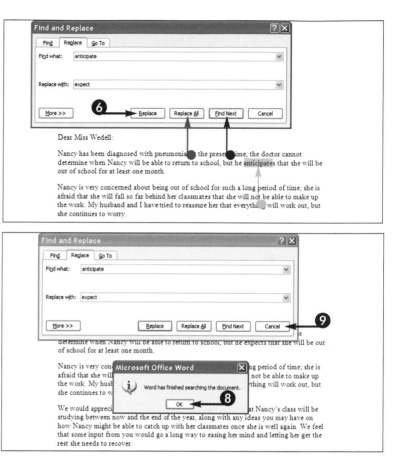

 TIPS

Can I find italic text and change it to boldface text?

Yes. Follow Steps **1** to **2** and click **More** to expand the window. Follow Steps **3** to **4**, but, instead of typing text, click **Format** and then click **Font**. In the Font style list of the Font dialog box that appears, click **Italic** for Step **3** and **Bold** for Step **4**. Then complete Steps **5** to **9**.

Can I search for and replace special characters such as tabs or paragraph marks?

Yes. Follow Steps **1** to **2** and click **More** to expand the window. Then, follow Steps **3** to **4**, but instead of typing text, click **Special** to display a menu of special characters. For Step **3**, select the special character you want to find. For Step **4**, select the special character you want to substitute. Then complete Steps **5** to **9**.

Count Words in a Document

You can count the number of words in a document or in any portion of a document. This is particularly handy when you must limit the number of words in a section of a document. Make use of this feature when a work or school project requires a specific number of words.

DISPLAY THE WORD COUNT

① Right-click the status bar.

The Status Bar Configuration menu appears.

● The number across from Word Count is the number of words in the document.

② If no check appears beside Word Count, click **Word Count**; otherwise, skip this step.

③ Click anywhere outside the menu.

● Word closes the menu and the number of words in the document appears on the status bar.

DISPLAY COUNT STATISTICS

1 Click the word count on the status bar.

The Word Count dialog box appears.

The Word Count dialog box reports the number of pages, words, characters with and without spaces, paragraphs, and lines in your document.

2 When you finish reviewing count statistics, click **Close**.

TIP

Can I count the number of words in just one paragraph?

Yes. Do the following:

1 Select the text containing the words you want to count.

● The number of words, along with the total words in the document, appears in the Word Count box on the status bar.

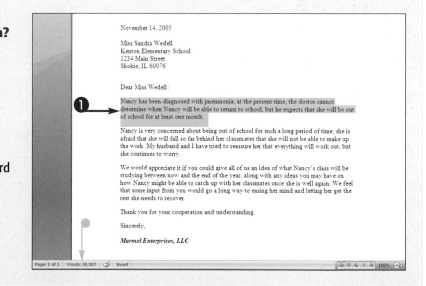

Correct Mistakes Automatically

Using the AutoCorrect feature, Word automatically corrects hundreds of common typing and spelling mistakes as you work. You can also add your own set of mistakes and the corrections to the list Word references.

① Click the **Office** icon (🔵).

② Click **Word Options**.

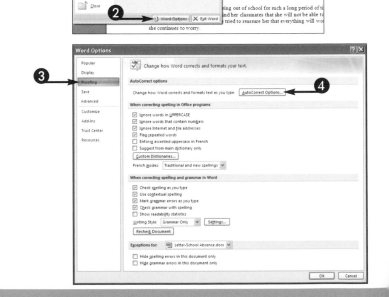

The Word Options dialog box appears.

③ Click **Proofing** to display proofing options.

④ Click **AutoCorrect Options**.

The AutoCorrect dialog box appears.

● The corrections Word already makes automatically appear in this area.

5 Click here and type the word you typically mistype or misspell.

6 Click here and type the correct version of the word.

7 Click **Add**.

● Word adds the entry to the list of entries to automatically correct.

You can repeat Steps **5** to **7** for each automatic correction you want to add.

8 Click **OK** to close the AutoCorrect dialog box.

9 Click **OK** to close the Word Options dialog box.

How does the automatic correction work?

You do not need to do anything unusual – just type. If you mistype or misspell a word stored as an AutoCorrect entry, Word corrects the entry when you press Spacebar , Tab , or Enter .

What should I do if Word automatically replaces an entry that I do not want replaced?

Position the insertion point at the beginning of the AutoCorrected word and click the **AutoCorrect Options** icon ( ) that appears. From the list of choices displayed, click **Change back to**. To make Word permanently stop correcting an entry, follow Steps **1** to **4**, click the stored AutoCorrect entry in the list, and then click **Delete**.

Insert Frequently Used Text Automatically

Using the Quick Parts feature, you can store and then insert phrases you use frequently. The Quick Parts feature is particularly useful for phrases that take up more than one line, such as a name, title, and company name that appears at the bottom of a letter.

Quick Parts replace AutoText entries from earlier versions of Word. Any AutoText entries you created in earlier versions appear in Word 2007, but, unless you remember their names, you can insert them only using the Building Blocks Organizer window. For Word 2007, Quick Parts are faster and easier to use.

Insert Frequently Used Text Automatically

CREATE A QUICK PART ENTRY

1 Type the text that you want to store, including all formatting that should appear each time you insert the entry.

2 Select the text you typed.

3 Click the **Insert** tab.

4 Click **Quick Parts**.

5 Click **Save Selection to Quick Part Gallery**.

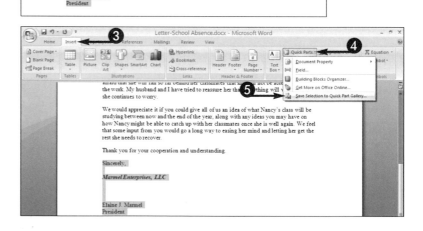

The Create New Building Block dialog box appears.

6 Type a name that you would like to use as a shortcut for the entry.

7 Click **OK**.

Word stores the entry on the Quick Parts Gallery.

INSERT A QUICK PART ENTRY

1 Position the insertion point where you want the Quick Part entry to appear.

2 Click **Quick Parts**.

● All building blocks you define as Quick Parts appear on the Quick Parts Gallery.

3 Click the entry.

Word inserts the Quick Part entry.

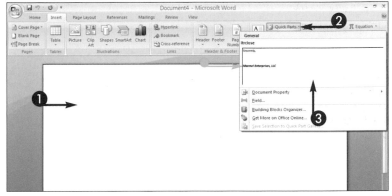

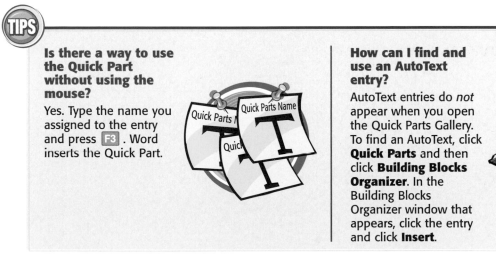

TIPS

Is there a way to use the Quick Part without using the mouse?

Yes. Type the name you assigned to the entry and press **F3** . Word inserts the Quick Part.

How can I find and use an AutoText entry?

AutoText entries do *not* appear when you open the Quick Parts Gallery. To find an AutoText, click **Quick Parts** and then click **Building Blocks Organizer**. In the Building Blocks Organizer window that appears, click the entry and click **Insert**.

Check Spelling and Grammar

Using the Spelling and Grammar Checker, you can search for and correct all spelling and grammar mistakes in your document. On-screen, Word places a red squiggly underline beneath spelling errors and a green squiggly underline beneath grammar errors.

Word does not identify a misspelling when a word is correctly spelled but misused; for example, if you type "their" when it should be "there," Word does not flag it as a misspelling.

Check Spelling and Grammar

① Click the **Review** tab.

② Click **Spelling and Grammar**.

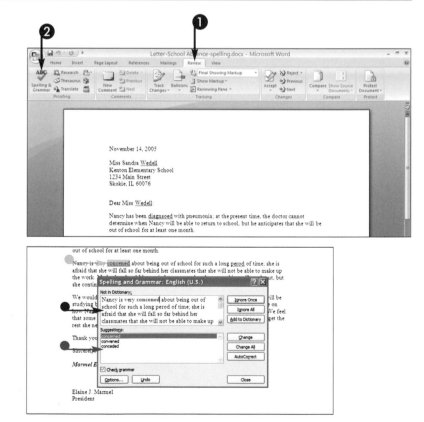

● Word selects the first spelling or grammar mistake and displays the Spelling and Grammar window.

Note: *If your document contains no errors, this window does not appear.*

● This area displays the spelling or grammar mistake.

● This area displays suggestions to correct the error.

③ Click the suggestion you want to use.

④ Click **Change**.

● You can click **Ignore Once** or **Ignore All** to leave the selected word or phrase unchanged.

Word selects the next spelling or grammar mistake.

⑤ Repeat Steps **3** to **4** for each spelling or grammar mistake.

Word displays a dialog box when it finishes checking for spelling and grammar mistakes.

⑥ Click **OK**.

Can I correct spelling and grammar mistakes as I work instead of checking them all at once?

Yes. Each time you see a red or green squiggly underline, right-click the word or phrase. Word displays a menu of suggestions; you can click one to correct the error.

When should I use the Add to Dictionary button?

Word identifies misspellings by comparing words in your document to its own dictionary. When a word you type does not appear in Word's dictionary, Word flags the word as misspelled. If the word is a term you use regularly, click **Add to Dictionary** so that Word stops flagging the word as a misspelling.

Disable Grammar and Spell Checking

If the red and green squiggly underlines annoy you, you can turn off automatic spelling and grammar checking.

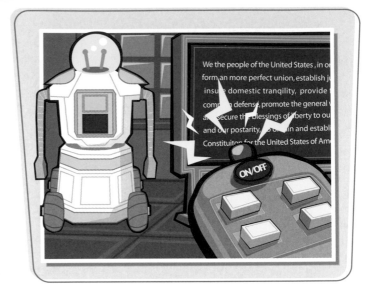

1 Click .

2 Click **Word Options**.

The Word Options dialog box appears.

3 Click **Proofing**.

4 Deselect the **Check spelling as you type** option (☑ changes to ☐) to disable automatic spell checking.

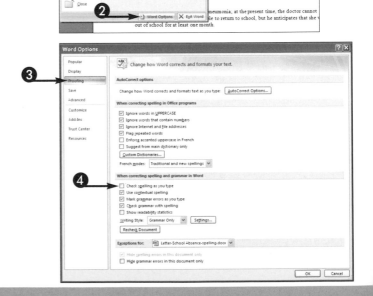

⑤ Deselect the **Mark grammar errors as you type** option (☑ changes to ☐) to disable automatic grammar checking.

⑥ Click **OK**.

● Word no longer identifies the spelling and grammar errors in your document.

November 14, 2005

Miss Sandra Wedell
Kenton Elementary School
1234 Main Street
Skokie, IL 60076

Dear Miss Wedell:

Nancy has been diagnsoed with pneumonia; at the present time, the doctor cannot determine when Nancy will be able to return to school, but he anticipates that she will be out of school for at least one month.

Nancy is very concened about being out of school for such a long perod of time; she is afraid that she will fall so far behind her classmates that she will not be able to make up the work. My husband and I have tried to reassure her that everything will work out, but she continues to worry.

 TIPS

If I disable automatic spelling and grammar checking, is there a way to check spelling and grammar?

Yes. Use the procedure described in the section "Check Spelling and Grammar." When you follow the procedure in the section "Disable Grammar and Spell Checking," you are disabling only the portion of the feature where Word automatically identifies misspellings or grammar mistakes with squiggly red or green underlines.

What should I do if I change my mind and decide that I want to see the red and green squiggly lines?

Repeat the steps in this section, selecting the boxes you deselected previously (☐ changes to ☑).

Find a Synonym or Antonym with the Thesaurus

Using the thesaurus, you can search for a more suitable word than the word you originally chose.

The thesaurus can help you find a synonym – a word with a similar meaning – for the word you originally chose, as well as an antonym – a word with an opposite meaning.

Find a Synonym or Antonym with the Thesaurus

① Click the word for which you want to find an opposite or substitute.

② Click the **Review** tab.

③ Click **Thesaurus**.

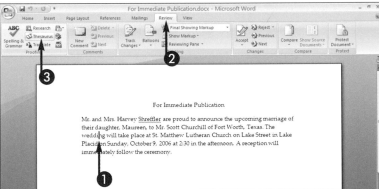

The Research task pane appears.

● The word you selected appears here.

● Click here to display a list of resources you can use to search for information.

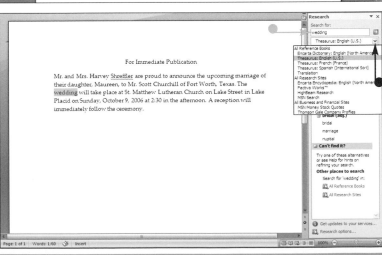

The Research pane contains a list of words with similar meanings appears.

● Each bold word represents a part of speech — a noun, a verb, an adjective — with a similar meaning to the word you selected.

● Each word listed below a bold word is a synonym for the bold word.

● Antonyms are marked.

④ Point the mouse at the word you want to use in your document.

☑ appears beside the word.

⑤ Click here to display a list of choices.

⑥ Click **Insert**.

Word replaces the word in your document with the one appearing in the Research task pane.

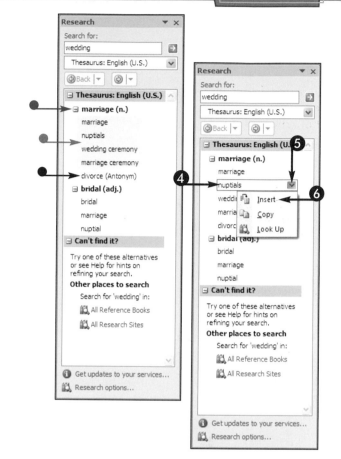

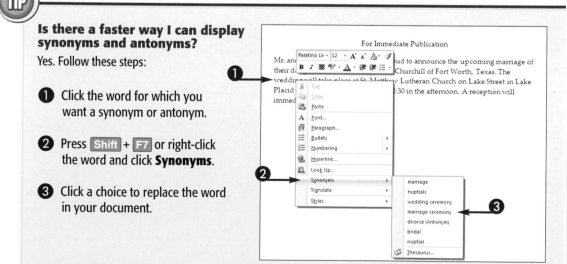

TIP

Is there a faster way I can display synonyms and antonyms?

Yes. Follow these steps:

❶ Click the word for which you want a synonym or antonym.

❷ Press Shift + F7 or right-click the word and click **Synonyms**.

❸ Click a choice to replace the word in your document.

Research
Information

Using the Research task pane, you can look up a word in the dictionary or search online resources for information on a variety of subjects using encyclopedias or online business resources.

Using online resources, you can search for essential business news and information to help you make better decisions faster, and you can get a stock quote.

Research Information

① Click a word in your document that you want to research.

② Click the **Review** tab.

③ Click **Research**.

The Research task pane appears.

● The word you clicked in Step **1** appears here.

④ Click here to display a list of resources available for research.

⑤ Click the resource you want to use.

Note: This example uses MSN Money Stock Quotes.

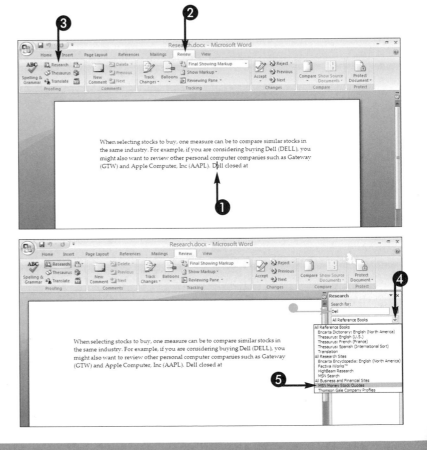

● Information from the research tool you selected appears in the Research task pane.

● Some of the research tools offer you a way to include the research in your document; for example, using MSN Money Stock Quotes, you can click ▼ and then click **Insert**.

TIPS

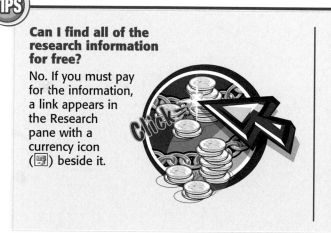

Can I find all of the research information for free?

No. If you must pay for the information, a link appears in the Research pane with a currency icon (▤) beside it.

How can Factiva iWorks help me?

Factiva iWorks provides free Web search capabilities and is designed to provide access to content that helps employees make quicker, more informed business decisions. It is a streamlined version of Factiva.com, the fee-based search engine built into Microsoft Office 2007.

Add Comments to a Document

You can add comments to clarify your documents. For example, you can use a comment to explain a statement, add a note of clarification, or remind you to take an action.

Add Comments to a Document

ADD A COMMENT

1 On the status bar, click the **Full Screen Reading** icon (📖), the **Web Layout** icon (📄), or the **Print Layout** icon (📄) to view your document.

   You alternatively can click 📖, 📄, or 📄 on the View tab.

2 Select the text about which you want to comment.

3 Click the **Review** tab.

4 Click **New Comment**.

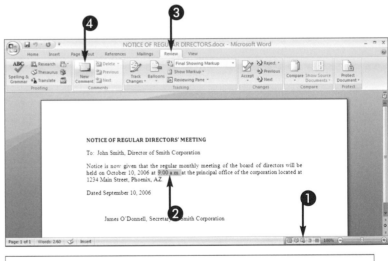

● A comment balloon appears in the markup area on the right side of the document.

● The comment balloon is attached to the text you selected, which is highlighted in the color of the balloon.

Note: In the comment, Word inserts the initials stored in the Personalize section of the Word Options dialog box.

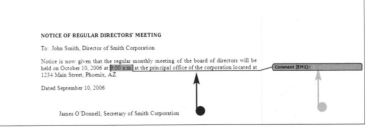

⑤ Type the text you want to store in the comment.

⑥ Click outside the comment balloon to save your comment.

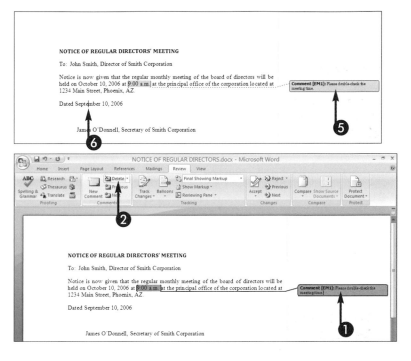

DELETE A COMMENT

① Click anywhere in the comment balloon you want to delete.

② In the Review tab, click **Delete**.

Word deletes the comment balloon and removes the highlighting from the associated text.

TIP

Can I insert a comment in Draft view or Outline view?

Yes. Do the following:

① Follow Steps **1** to **4** in this section, selecting **Draft** view (▢) or **Outline** view (▢) in Step **1**.

A pane containing the insertion point appears on the left side of the screen.

② Type your comment.

③ To continue working, click in the document.

● To hide the pane, click the **Close** icon (☒).

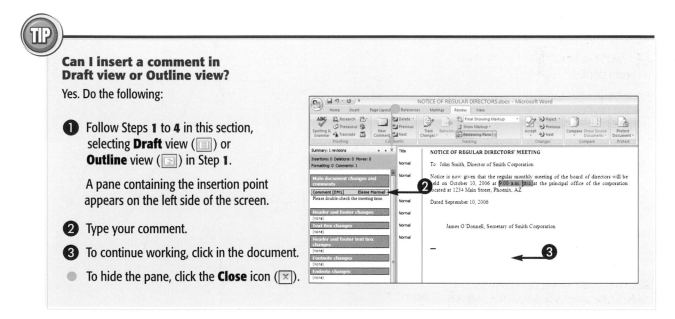

Track Document Changes During Review

Word can track the editing and formatting changes made to your document. This feature is particularly useful when more than one person works on the same document.

When Word tracks document revisions, it tracks the changes made and who made them so that you can easily identify who did what to a document.

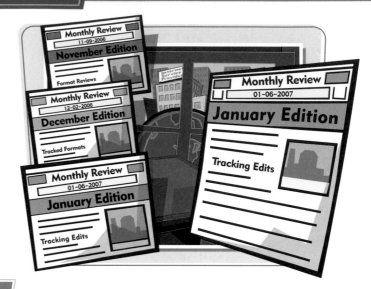

Track Document Changes During Review

1 Click 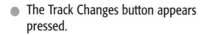.

The document appears in Print Layout view.

2 Click the **Review** tab.

3 Click **Track Changes**.

● The Track Changes button appears pressed.

4 Make changes to the document as needed.

● A vertical bar appears in the left margin beside lines containing changes.

● Deleted text changes appear with strikethrough formatting.

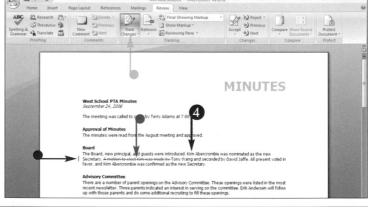

● Added text appears underlined and in a color other than black.

Each reviewer's changes appear in a different color.

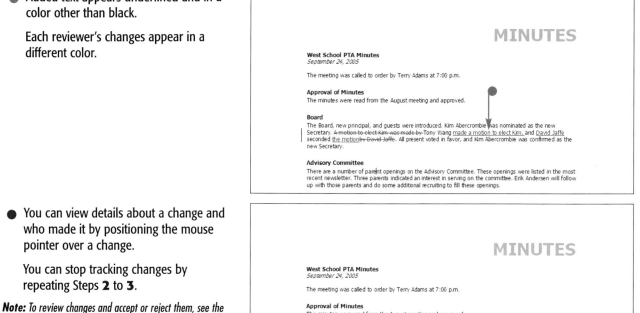

● You can view details about a change and who made it by positioning the mouse pointer over a change.

You can stop tracking changes by repeating Steps **2** to **3**.

Note: To review changes and accept or reject them, see the section "Review Tracked Changes."

TIPS

Can I print revisions?

Revisions will print as they appear on-screen. You can, however, print a list of revisions from any view.

❶ Click the **Office** icon ( ).

❷ Click **Print**.

❸ Click here and select **List of markup**.

❹ Click **OK**.

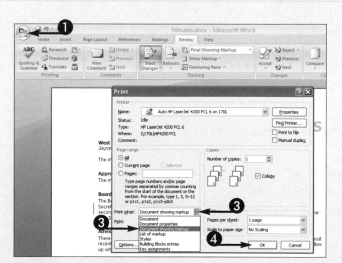

Review Tracked Changes

When you review a document containing tracked changes, you decide whether to accept or reject the changes. As you accept or reject changes, Word removes the revision marks.

Review Tracked Changes

① Open a document in which changes were tracked.

② Position the mouse pointer over any change to view details about it.

● Word displays the name of the person who made the change, the date and time of the change, and the details of the change.

③ Press **Ctrl** + **Home** to place the insertion point at the beginning of the document.

④ Click the **Review** tab.

⑤ Click **Next** to review the first change.

● Word highlights the change.

You can click **Next** again to skip over the change without accepting or rejecting it.

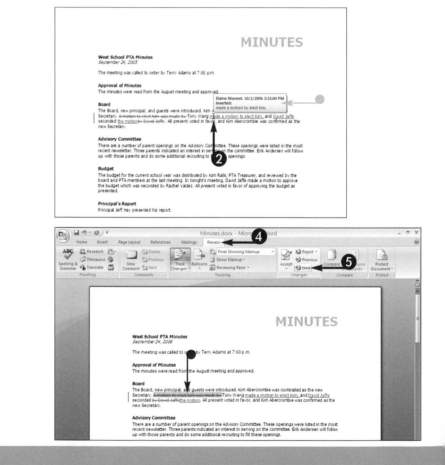

⑥ Click **Accept** to incorporate the change into the document or **Reject** to revert the text to its original state.

Word accepts or rejects the change, removes the revision marks, and highlights the next change.

⑦ Repeat Step **6** to review all revisions.

● If you need to move backwards to a change you previously skipped, you can click **Previous**.

When you have reviewed all changes, this dialog box appears.

⑧ Click **OK**.

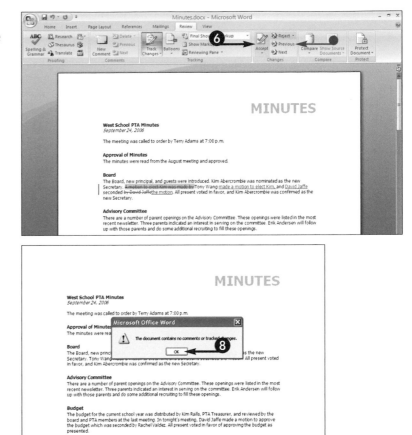

 TIP

Is there a way I can work in the document without addressing the changes or viewing the tracking marks?

You can work viewing the original document before changes or viewing the edited document after changes; in either case, you can hide the revision marks.

① Click the **Display for Review** button.

② Click **Final** to view the edited document without revision marks or click **Original** to view the document without revision marks, before any changes were made.

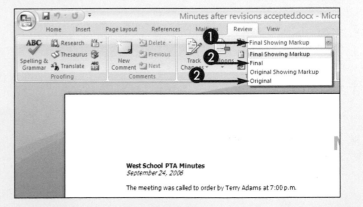

Combine Reviewers' Comments

You can combine two versions of the same document; this feature is particularly useful when two reviewers have each reviewed the same original and you want to work from the combined changes of both reviewers.

Combine Reviewers' Comments

① Click the **Review** tab.

② Click **Compare**.

③ Click **Combine**.

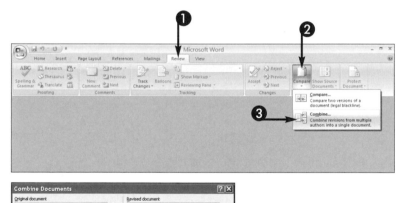

The Combine Documents dialog box appears.

④ Click the **Open** icon (📂) beside the Original document ▾.

The Open dialog box appears.

⑤ Navigate to the folder containing the original file you want to combine.

⑥ Click the file.

⑦ Click **Open**.

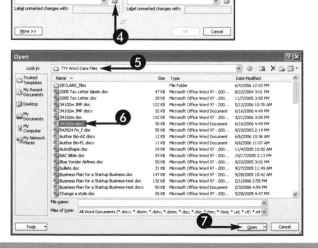

The Combine Documents dialog box reappears.

8 Repeat Steps **4** to **7**, clicking the 📷 beside the Revised document ⬇.

● You can type a label for changes to each document in these boxes.

9 Click **OK**.

Word displays four panes.

● The left pane summarizes revisions.

● The middle pane contains the results of combining the original document and the reviewed document.

● The top right pane displays the original document.

● The bottom right pane displays the reviewed document.

TIP

What happens when I click the More button?

Word displays a series of settings you can control. You can specify the comparisons you want to make and you can identify how to show changes. To change your settings, follow these steps:

1 Click the options that you want.

● You can select comparison settings in this area (☐ changes to ☑).

● You can select the changes that you want to see in this area (○ changes to ⦿).

2 Click **OK**.

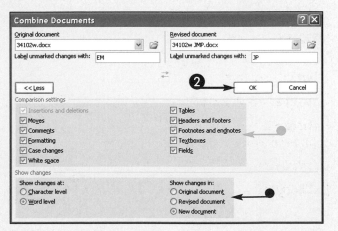

Format Text

You can format text for emphasis and for greater readability. And, although the individual types of formatting are discussed separately, you can perform each of the tasks in this chapter on a single selection of text.

You can change the typeface that appears in your document by changing the font. Changing the font can help readers better understand your document. Microsoft has added 13 new TrueType fonts to Word 2007.

Use serif fonts – fonts with short lines stemming from the bottoms of the letters – to provide a line that helps guide the reader's eyes. Use sans serif fonts – fonts without short lines stemming from the bottoms of the letters – for headlines.

Change the Font

① Select the text that you want to change to a different font.

The Mini Toolbar appears faded in the background.

You can use the Mini Toolbar by moving ⇲ up toward the Mini Toolbar.

● To use the Ribbon, you can click the **Home** tab.

② Click here to display a list of the available fonts on your computer.

● If you use the Ribbon, Word displays a sample of the selected text in any font at which you point the mouse.

Note: See Chapter 1 for details on Live Preview.

③ Click the font you want to use.

Word assigns the font you selected to the text you selected.

You can click anywhere outside the selection to continue working.

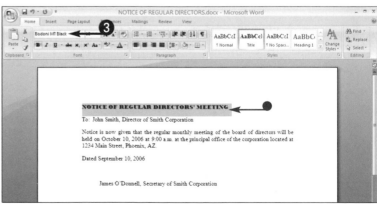

You can increase or decrease the size of the text in your document. Increase the size to make reading the text easier; decrease the size to fit more text on a page.

Change Text Size

① Select the text that you want to assign a new size.

The Mini Toolbar appears faded in the background.

You can use the Mini Toolbar by moving ▷ up toward the Mini Toolbar.

● To use the Ribbon, click the **Home** tab.

② Click here to display a list of the possible sizes for the current font.

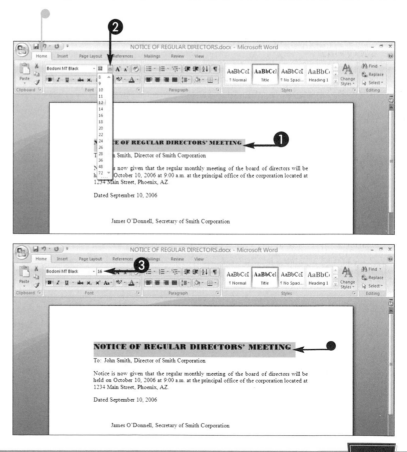

● If you use the Ribbon, Word displays a sample of the selected text in any font size at which you point the mouse.

Note: See Chapter 1 for details on Live Preview.

③ Click the size you want to use.

Word changes the size of the selected text.

You can click anywhere outside the selection to continue working.

Emphasize Information with Bold, Italic, or Underline

You can apply italics, boldface, or underlining to text in your document for emphasis.

Emphasize Information with Bold, Italic, or Underline

① Select the text that you want to emphasize.

● The Mini Toolbar appears faded in the background.

You can use the Mini Toolbar by moving ▷ up toward the Mini Toolbar.

● If you want to use the Ribbon, click the **Home** tab.

② Click the **Bold** icon (B), the **Italic** icon (I), or the **Underline** icon (U) on the Ribbon or the Mini Toolbar.

● Word applies the emphasis you selected.

You can click anywhere outside the selection to continue working.

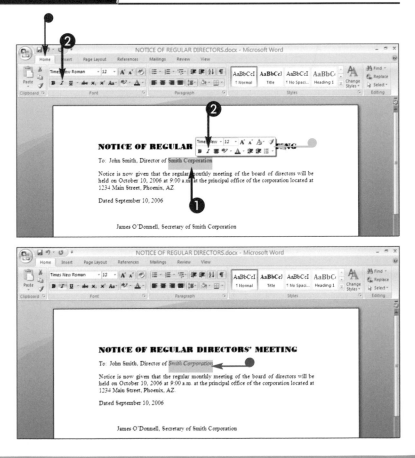

You can assign superscript or subscript notation to any text to make it appear above or below the regular line of text. Superscripting and subscripting are often used when inserting trademark symbols.

The example in this section uses superscript.

Superscript or Subscript Text

① Type the text that you want to superscript or subscript.

② Select the text that you want to superscript or subscript.

The Mini Toolbar appears faded in the background.

③ Click the **Home** tab.

④ Click the **Superscript** icon (x¹) or the **Subscript** icon (x₂).

● Word superscripts or subscripts the selected text.

You can click anywhere outside the selection to continue working.

Change Text Case

You can change the case of selected text instead of retyping it with a new case applied.

Change Text Case

① Select the text that you want to assign a new case.

The Mini Toolbar appears faded in the background.

② Click the **Home** tab.

③ Click the **Change Case** icon (Aa).

④ Click the case you want to use.

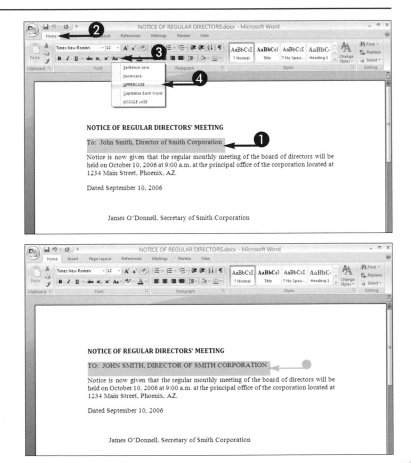

● The selected text appears in the new case.

You can click anywhere outside the selection to continue working.

Change Text Color

You can change the color of selected text for emphasis. Color is effective when you view your document on-screen, save it to a pdf or an xps file, or print it using a color printer.

Change Text Color

① Select the text that you want to change to a different color.

● The Mini Toolbar appears faded in the background.

You can use the Mini Toolbar by moving ⇖ up toward the Mini Toolbar.

● To use the Ribbon, click the **Home** tab.

② Click the **Font Color** icon (▲) on the Ribbon or on the Mini Toolbar and point at a color.

If you use the Ribbon, Word displays a sample of the selected text.

Note: See Chapter 1 for details on Live Preview.

③ Click a color.

● Word assigns the color to the selected text.

You can click anywhere outside the selection to continue working.

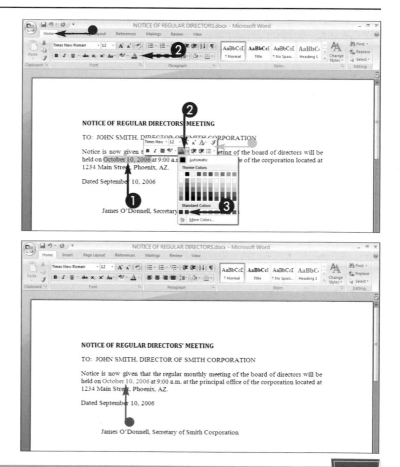

Apply Highlighting to Text

You can use color to create highlights in a document to draw attention to the text. Highlighting is effective when you view the document on-screen or when you print it using a color printer.

Apply Highlighting to Text

① Select the text that you want to highlight.

The Mini Toolbar appears faded in the background.

You can use the Mini Toolbar by moving ▷ up toward the Mini Toolbar.

② To use the Ribbon, click the **Home** tab.

③ Click the **Text Highlight Color** icon (🔲) on the Ribbon or the Mini Toolbar and point at a color.

If you use the Ribbon, Word displays a sample of the selected text highlighted in any color at which you point the mouse.

Note: See Chapter 1 for details on Live Preview.

④ Click a color.

● Word highlights the selected text using the color you chose.

You can click anywhere outside the selection to continue working.

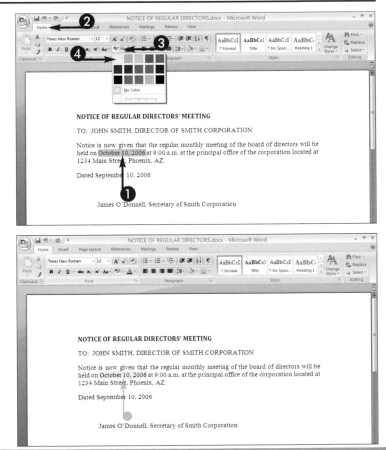

To save time, you can copy formatting that you apply to text in one portion of your document to another portion of your document.

Copy Text Formatting

1 Select the text containing the formatting that you want to copy.

● The Mini Toolbar appears faded in the background.

You can use the Mini Toolbar by moving ⬉ up toward the Mini Toolbar.

● To use the Ribbon, click the **Home** tab.

2 Click the **Format Painter** icon (🖌).

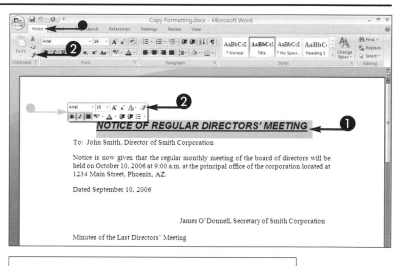

The mouse pointer changes to 🖌I when you move the mouse over your document.

3 Select the text to which you want to assign formatting.

The newly selected text changes to the format used for the original selection.

You can click anywhere outside the selection to continue working.

Remove Text Formatting

You can quickly and easily remove formatting that you have applied to text in your document.

Remove Text Formatting

① Select the text from which you want to remove formatting.

The Mini Toolbar appears faded in the background.

② Click the **Home** tab.

③ Click the **Clear Formatting** icon (![icon]).

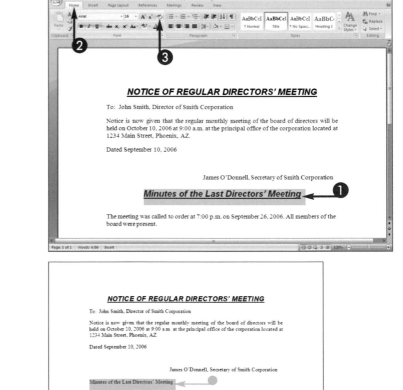

● Word removes all formatting from the selected text.

Click anywhere outside the selection to continue working.

Strikethrough formatting is often used in the legal community to identify text the reviewer proposes to delete.

If you need to track both additions and deletions and want to update the document in an automated way, use Word's review tracking features as described in Chapter 4.

Apply Strikethrough to Text

1 Select the text to which you want to apply strikethrough formatting.

The Mini Toolbar appears faded in the background.

2 Click the **Home** tab.

3 Click the **Strikethrough** icon (abc).

● Word applies strikethrough formatting to the selected text.

You can click anywhere outside the selection to continue working.

You can repeat these steps to remove strikethrough formatting.

NOTICE OF REGULAR DIRECTORS' MEETING

To: John Smith, Director of Smith Corporation

Notice is now given that the regular monthly meeting of the board of directors will be held on October 10, 2006 at 9:00 a.m. at the principal office of the corporation located at 1234 Main Street, Phoenix, AZ.

Dated September 10, 2006

es O'Donnell, Secretary of Smith Corporation

Minutes of the Last Directors' Meeting

The meeting was called to order at 7:00 p.m. on September 26, 2006. All members of the board were present.

NOTICE OF REGULAR DIRECTORS' MEETING

To: John Smith, Director of Smith Corporation

Notice is now given that the regular monthly meeting of the board of directors will be held on October 10, 2006 at 9:00 a.m. at the principal office of the corporation located at 1234 Main Street, Phoenix, AZ.

Dated September 10, 2006

James O'Donnell, Secretary of Smith Corporation

Minutes of the Last Directors' Meeting

The meeting was called to order at 7:00 p.m. on September 26, 2006. All members of the board were present.

Set the Default Font for All New Documents

You can change the default font that Word uses for all new documents you create. The default font that ships with Word is Calibri, 11 point.

Changing the default font does not affect documents you have already created.

1 Click the **Home** tab.

2 Right-click the Normal style.

3 Click **Modify**.

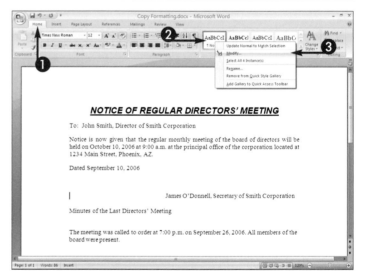

The Modify Style dialog box appears.

4 Click in these areas to select the font and font size that you want to use for all new documents.

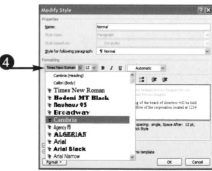

● A preview of the new settings appears here.

5 Click the **New documents based on this template** option (○ changes to ◉).

6 Click **OK**.

● Word changes the default font in the open document.

When you open a new document, the default font will be the font you selected.

Note: *To open a new document, see Chapter 2.*

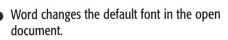

NOTICE OF REGULAR DIRECTORS' MEETING

To: John Smith, Director of Smith Corporation

Notice is now given that the regular monthly meeting of the board of directors will be held on October 10, 2006 at 9:00 a.m. at the principal office of the corporation located at 1234 Main Street, Phoenix, AZ.

Dated September 10, 2006

James O'Donnell, Secretary of Smith Corporation

Minutes of the Last Directors' Meeting

The meeting was called to order at 7:00 p.m. on September 26, 2006. All members of the board were present.

TIP

How can I indent the first line of each paragraph by default?

Follow these steps:

1 Complete Steps **1** to **5**.

2 Click **Format** and, from the list that appears, click **Paragraph**.

3 Click here and click **First line**.

4 Click **OK** twice.

Format Paragraphs

Instead of formatting individual words in your document, you can apply changes to entire paragraphs to help certain sections of your text stand out. You can apply formatting such as line spacing, bullets, or borders to the paragraphs in your document to enhance the appearance of the document.

You can change the alignment of various paragraphs in your document to enhance the document's appearance.

You can align text with the left or right margins, center it between the left and right margins, or justify it so that the text aligns with both the left and right margins. To align text vertically, see Chapter 7.

Change Text Alignment

① Select the text that you want to align.

② Click the **Home** tab.

③ Click an alignment option.

The **Align Left** icon (▤) aligns text with the left margin, the **Center** icon (▤), centers it between the left and right margins, the **Align Right** icon (▤) aligns it with the right margin, and the **Justify** icon (▤) aligns text with both the left and right margins.

Note: *This example centers a headline between the left and right margins.*

Word aligns the text.

④ Click anywhere outside the selection to continue working.

● This text is aligned with the left margin.

● This text is centered between both margins.

● This text is aligned with the right margin.

● This text is justified between both margins.

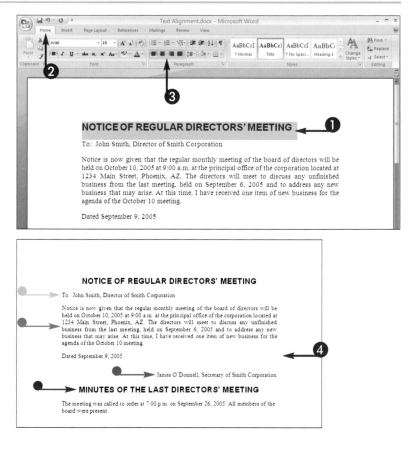

You can change the amount of space Word places between the lines of text within a paragraph. Word 2007 uses a different default line spacing than Word 2003 and earlier.

Word can measure line spacing in inches, but it is typically easiest to measure in points, specified as pts. 12 pts equals approximately one line of space.

Set Line Spacing Within a Paragraph

① Select at least two lines of text to which you want to apply line spacing.

② Click **Home**.

③ Click the **Line Spacing** icon ([≡]).

④ Click a number.

1 is for single spacing, the default in Word 97–2003; or **1.15** is the new default spacing in Word 2007; **1.5** places 1/2 blank line between lines of text; **2** represents double spacing; **2.5** places 1–1/2 blank lines between lines of text; and **3** represents triple spacing.

● Word applies the line spacing you specified to the selected text.

⑤ Click anywhere outside the selection to continue working.

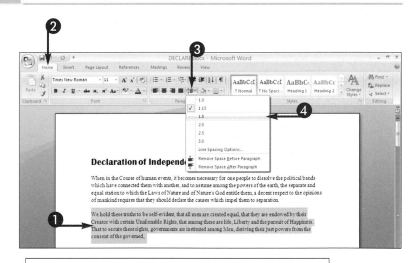

Set Line Spacing Between Paragraphs

You can change the amount of space Word places between paragraphs of text. For example, you can use this technique to set double spacing between paragraphs while maintaining single spacing within each paragraph.

By default, Word 2007 uses different settings than Word 2003 and earlier for space between paragraphs.

1 Select the paragraph or paragraphs for which you want to define spacing.

2 Click the **Home** tab.

3 Click the **Paragraph** 🔲.

The Paragraph dialog box appears.

4 Click here to increase or decrease the space before the selected paragraph.

5 Click here to increase or decrease the space after the selected paragraph.

6 Click **OK**.

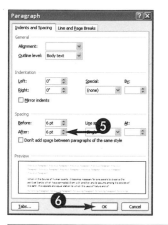

● Word applies the spacing before and after the selected paragraph.

7 Click anywhere outside the selection to continue working.

Declaration of Independence

When in the Course of human events, it becomes necessary for one people to dissolve the political bands which have connected them with another, and to assume among the powers of the earth, the separate and equal station to which the Laws of Nature and of Nature's God entitle them, a decent respect to the opinions of mankind requires that they should declare the causes which impel them to separation.

We hold these truths to be self-evident, that all men are created equal, that they are endowed by their Creator with certain Unalienable Rights, that among these are life, Liberty and the pursuit of Happiness. That to secure these rights, governments are instituted among Men, deriving their just powers from the consent of the governed,

That whenever any form of Government becomes destructive of these ends, it is the right of the People to alter or to abolish it and to institute a new Government, laying its foundation on such principles and organizing its power in such form, as to them shall seem most likely to affect their Safety and Happiness. Prudence, indeed, will dictate that Governments long established should not be changed for light and transient causes; and accordingly all experience has shown, that mankind is more disposed to suffer, which evils are sufferable, than to right themselves by abolishing the forms to which they are accustomed. But when a long train of abuses and usurpations, pursuing invariably the same Object evinces a design to reduce them under absolute Despotism, it is their right, it is their duty, to throw off such Government, and to provide new Guards for their future security.

Such has been the patient sufferance of these colonies; and such is now the necessity which constrains them to alter their former Systems of Government. The history of the present King of Great Britain is a history of repeated injuries and usurpations, all having in direct object the establishment of an absolute Tyranny over these States. To prove this, let Facts be submitted to a candid world.

TIPS

Is there a way that I can use Word 2003 and earlier spacing?

Yes. On the Home tab, click the **Change Styles** button, point to **Style Sets**, and click **Traditional** to set line spacing within a paragraph to single spacing and line spacing between paragraphs to 0.

How many points should I use before and after paragraphs to leave one blank line between paragraphs?

Assign 6 points before and after each paragraph. The 6 points of space at the bottom of Paragraph 1 plus the 6 points of space at the top of Paragraph 2 equals 12 points, or one line space. A point is 1/72nd of an inch. A 72-point line of text is approximately 1 inch high. Measure 1 inch of text vertically; in most cases, six lines of text fill 1 vertical inch of space. One line equals about 1/6 of an inch, and 1/6 of an inch equals 12 points of vertical line space.

Create a Bulleted or Numbered List

You can use bullets or numbers to call attention to lists that you present in your documents.

Use numbers when the items in your list follow a particular order. Use bullets when the items in your list do not follow any particular order.

CREATE A LIST FROM EXISTING TEXT

1. Select the text to which you want to assign bullets or numbers.

2. Click the **Home** tab.

3. Click the **Numbering** icon (▤) or the **Bullets** icon (▤).

   You can find ▤ on the Mini Toolbar.

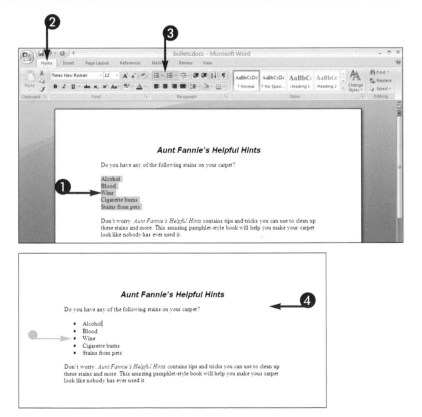

● Word applies numbers or bullets to the selection.

4. Click anywhere outside the selection to continue working.

CREATE A LIST AS YOU TYPE

1 Type **1.** to create a numbered list or ***** to create a bulleted list.

2 Press **Spacebar** or **Tab**.

To Do List:

1.|

1

Word automatically formats the entry as a list item and displays the AutoCorrect Options button so that you can undo or stop automatic numbering.

3 Type a list item.

4 Press **Enter** to prepare to type another list item.

● Word automatically adds a bullet or number for the next list item.

5 Repeat Steps **2** to **3** for each list item.

To stop entering items in the list, press **Enter** twice.

To Do List:

1. Call Holly Reed ◄——— **3**
2. |

TIP

Can I create a bulleted or numbered list with more than one level, like the type of list you use when creating an outline?

Yes, using the **Multilevel** List icon ( ).

1 Click .

2 Click a format.

3 Type your list.

● You can press **Enter** to enter a new list item at the same list level.

● Each time you press **Tab**, Word indents a level in the list.

● Each time you press **Shift** + **Tab**, Word outdents a level in the list.

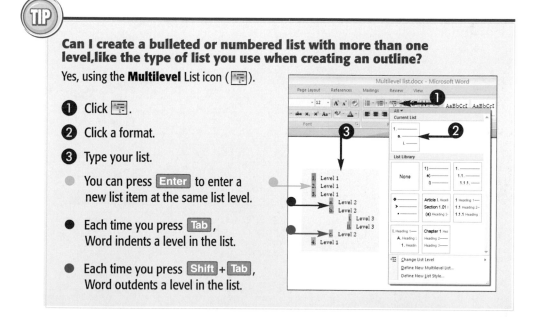

Display Formatting Marks

You can display formatting marks that do not print but help you identify formatting in your document.

Word can display formatting marks that represent spaces, tabs, paragraphs, hidden text, and optional hyphens.

❶ Open any document.

❷ Click the **Home** tab.

❸ Click the **Show/Hide** icon (¶).

Word displays all formatting marks in your document.

● Single dots (.) appear each time you press Spacebar ; paragraph marks (¶) appear each time you press Enter ; and arrows (→) appear each time you press Tab .

● Hidden text appears underlined with dots.

● Optional hyphens, inserted by pressing Ctrl + - , appear as ¬.

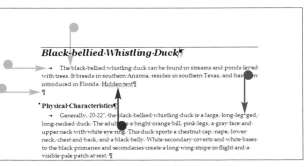

You can hide or display horizontal and vertical rulers to help you identify the position of the insertion point or to align text.

You can use the ruler to indent paragraphs or set tabs in your document; see the sections "Indent Paragraphs" and "Set Tabs" in this chapter.

Hide or Display the Ruler

① Click the **View** tab.

② Click **Ruler**.

● Rulers appear below the Ribbon and on the left side of your document.

● You can click the **Ruler** icon (⬚) to hide or display the ruler.

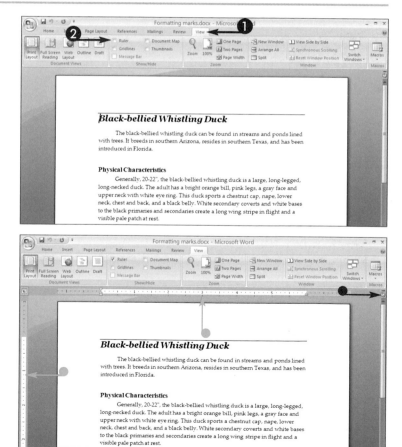

Indent Paragraphs

You can indent paragraphs in your document from the left and right margins. You also can indent only the first line of a paragraph or all lines *except* the first line of the paragraph.

① Select the text that you want to indent.

② Click the **Home** tab.

③ Click the **Paragraph** 🖻.

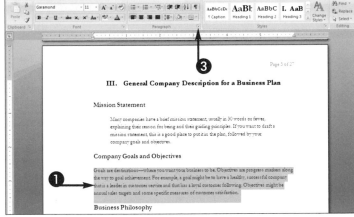

The Paragraph dialog box appears.

④ Click here to specify the number of inches to indent the left and right edge of the paragraph.

● The effects of your settings appear here.

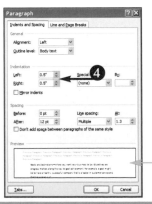

⑤ Click here and select an indenting option.

First line indents only the first line of the paragraph, and **Hanging** indents all lines *except* the first line of the paragraph.

⑥ Click here to set the amount of the first line or hanging indent.

● The effects of your settings appear here.

⑦ Click **OK**.

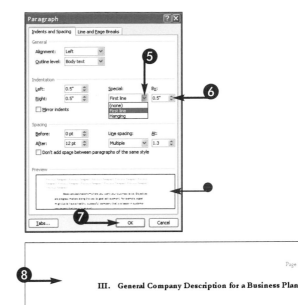

● Word applies your settings to the selected paragraph.

⑧ Click anywhere outside the selection to continue working.

III. General Company Description for a Business Plan

Mission Statement

Many companies have a brief mission statement, usually in 30 words or fewer, explaining their reason for being and their guiding principles. If you want to draft a mission statement, this is a good place to put it in the plan, followed by your company goals and objectives.

Company Goals and Objectives

Goals are destinations—where you want your business to be. Objectives are progress markers along the way to goal achievement. For example, a goal might be to have a healthy, successful company that is a leader in customer service and that has a loyal customer following. Objectives might be annual sales targets and some specific measures of customer satisfaction.

Business Philosophy

TIPS

Can I set paragraph indentations without using a dialog box?

Yes. You can use buttons in the ruler. On the ruler, drag the **Left Indent** icon (▱) to indent all lines from the left margin, drag the **Hanging Indent** icon (▱) to create a hanging indent, or drag the **First Line Indent** icon (▽) to indent the first line only. On the right side of the ruler, drag ▱ to indent all lines from the right margin.

What do the Decrease Indent icon and the Increase Indent icon do?

The **Increase Indent** icon (▦) indents all lines from the left margin. The **Decrease Indent** icon (▦) decreases the indent of all lines from the left margin.

You can use left, center, right, decimal, or bar tabs to line up columnar information. Using tabs ensures that information lines up properly within a column.

By default, Word places tabs every .5 inch across the page between the left and right margins.

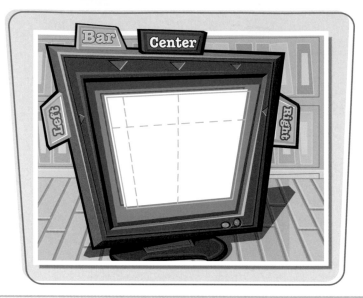

Set Tabs

ADD A TAB

1 Click here until the type of tab you want to add appears.

▫ Left tab

▫ Center tab

▫ Right tab

▫ Decimal tab

▫ Bar tab

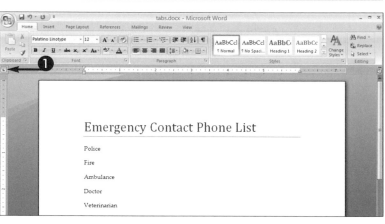

2 Select the lines to which you want to add a tab.

3 Click the ruler where you want the tab to appear.

Word displays a tab at the location you clicked on each selected line.

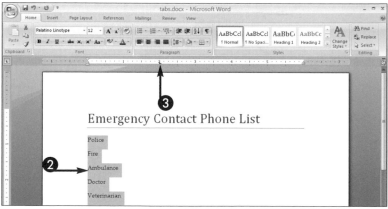

USING A TAB

① Click to the left of the information you want to appear at the tab.

② Press **Tab**.

③ Type your text.

The text appears at the tab.

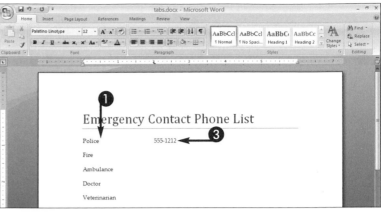

MOVE A TAB

① Click the line using the tab or select the lines of text affected by the tab.

② Drag the tab to the left or right.

● A vertical line marks its position as you drag.

When you click and drag a tab, the text moves with the tab.

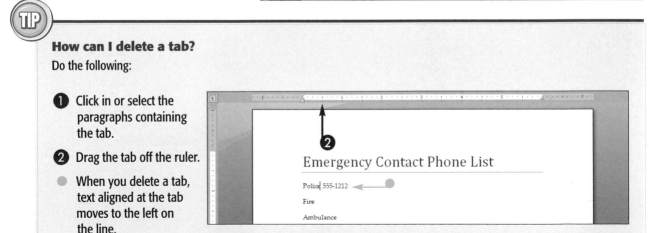

TIP

How can I delete a tab?
Do the following:

① Click in or select the paragraphs containing the tab.

② Drag the tab off the ruler.

● When you delete a tab, text aligned at the tab moves to the left on the line.

continued

You can use dot leader tabs to help your reader follow information across a page.

ADD LEADER CHARACTERS TO TABS

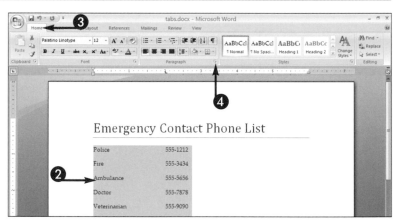

1. Follow Steps **1** to **3** in the "Add a Tab" subsection on the previous page to create a tab stop.

2. Select the text containing the tab to which you want to add dot leaders.

3. Click the **Home** tab.

4. Click the **Paragraph** 🔲.

The Paragraph dialog box appears.

5. Click **Tabs**.

The Tabs dialog box appears.

6 Click the tab setting to which you want to add leaders.

7 Click a type of leader (○ changes to ⊙).

8 Click **OK**.

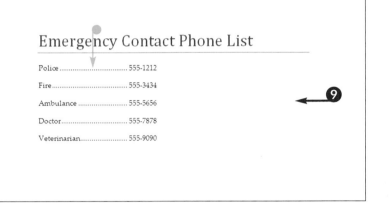

● Word adds leading characters from the last character before the tab to the first character at the tab.

9 Click anywhere outside the selection to continue working.

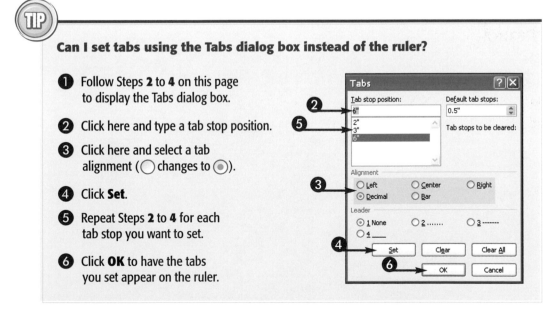

Emergency Contact Phone List

Police 555-1212

Fire 555-3434

Ambulance 555-5656

Doctor 555-7878

Veterinarian 555-9090

TIP

Can I set tabs using the Tabs dialog box instead of the ruler?

1 Follow Steps **2** to **4** on this page to display the Tabs dialog box.

2 Click here and type a tab stop position.

3 Click here and select a tab alignment (○ changes to ⊙).

4 Click **Set**.

5 Repeat Steps **2** to **4** for each tab stop you want to set.

6 Click **OK** to have the tabs you set appear on the ruler.

Add a Paragraph Border

You can draw attention to a paragraph containing important information by adding a border to it.

Add a Paragraph Border

① Select the text that you want to surround with a border.

② Click the **Home** tab.

③ Click here on the **Borders** icon (▦).

④ Click **Borders and Shading**.

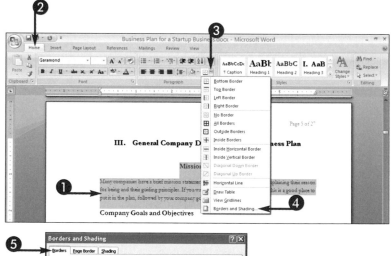

The Borders and Shading dialog box appears.

⑤ Click the **Borders** tab.

⑥ Click here to select a type of border.

This example uses Box.

7 Click here to select the style for the border line.

8 Click here and select a color for the border line.

9 Click here and select a thickness for the border line.

● This area shows the results of the settings you select.

10 Click **OK**.

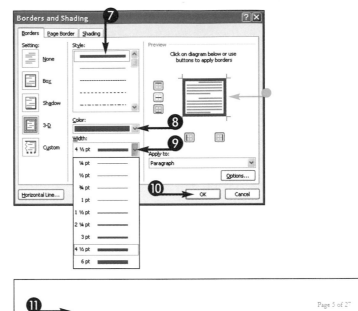

● The border appears around the selected text.

11 Click anywhere outside the selection to continue working.

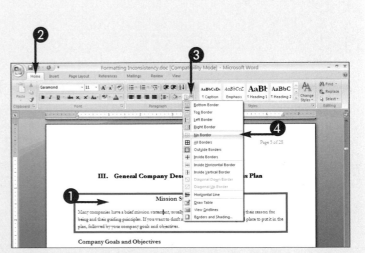

TIP

How do I remove a border?

Follow these steps below. If you are willing to usethe same color, style, and thickness of the border,you also can use the same steps to quickly apply aborder to any paragraph, clicking the type of borderyou want to apply in Step **4**.

1 Click anywhere in the text surrounded by a border.

2 Click the **Home** tab.

3 Click here on ▦.

4 Click **No Border**.

Word removes the border.

Check for Formatting Inconsistencies

You can have Word mark, with wavy blue underlines, text you have formatted inconsistently in your document. This feature is useful when you want to make sure that you have applied direct formatting, such as italics, consistently or that you have used styles whenever possible.

For each formatting inconsistency, Word suggests a way that you can make the formatting consistent and give your document a more professional-looking appearance.

Check for Formatting Inconsistencies

DISPLAY FORMAT INCONSISTENCIES

1 Click the **Office** icon ().

2 Click **Word Options**.

The Word Options dialog box appears.

3 Click **Advanced**.

4 In the Editing options section, click **Mark formatting inconsistencies** (☐ changes to ☑).

5 Click **OK**.

Word saves your settings.

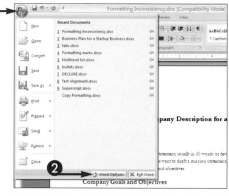

CORRECT FORMATTING INCONSISTENCIES

① Right-click a formatting inconsistency to display a menu.

● Formatting inconsistencies appear with wavy blue underlines.

② To correct the inconsistency, click the first option on the menu.

● You can ignore this inconsistency by clicking **Ignore Once**, or you can ignore all occurrences of this inconsistency by clicking **Ignore Rule**.

● Word selects the inconsistency, corrects or ignores it, and removes the wavy blue underline.

③ Click anywhere outside the selection to continue working.

④ Repeat Steps **1** to **2** for each inconsistency.

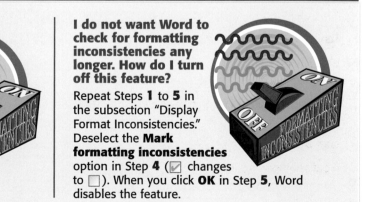

 TIPS

What kinds of formatting inconsistencies does Word check for?

Word looks for occurrences of similar, but not identical, formatting that you applied directly to text or lists. Word also looks for occurrences of formatting you applied directly to text that matches styles you applied elsewhere in your document.

I do not want Word to check for formatting inconsistencies any longer. How do I turn off this feature?

Repeat Steps **1** to **5** in the subsection "Display Format Inconsistencies." Deselect the **Mark formatting inconsistencies** option in Step **4** (☑ changes to ☐). When you click **OK** in Step **5**, Word disables the feature.

Review and Change Formatting

You can review the formatting associated with text in your document to see the details of exactly what formatting is applied to the text.

① Select the text containing the formatting you want to review.

② Click the **Home** tab.

③ Click the **Styles** (⬜).

The Styles task pane appears.

④ Click the **Style Inspector** icon (🔲).

The Style Inspector pane appears.

⑤ Click the **Reveal Formatting** icon (🔲).

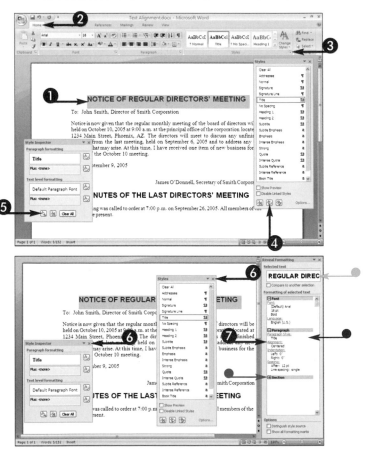

The Reveal Formatting pane appears.

⑥ Click the **Close** icons (☒) to close the Styles pane and the Style Inspector pane.

● A portion of the selected text appears here.

● Formatting details for the selected text appear here.

● You can click a plus sign (⊞) beside a bold heading in the Reveal Formatting pane to display links.

⑦ Click the link for the type of change you want to make.

In this example, the Indents and Spacing tab of the Paragraph dialog box appears.

8 Select the options you want to change.

9 Click **OK**.

● Word applies the formatting changes.

● The information in the Reveal Formatting task pane updates.

10 Click anywhere to continue working.

● You can click ☒ to close the Reveal Formatting task pane.

NOTICE OF REGULAR DIRECTORS' MEETING

To: John Smith, Director of Smith Corporation

Notice is now given that the regular monthly meeting of the board of directors will be held on October 10, 2005 at 9:00 a.m. at the principal office of the corporation located at 1234 Main Street, Phoenix, AZ. The directors will meet to discuss any unfinished business from the last meeting, held on September 6, 2005 and to address any new business that may arise. At this time, I have received one item of new business for the agenda of the October 10 meeting.

Dated September 9, 2005

James O'Donnell, Secretary of Smith Corporation

MINUTES OF THE LAST DIRECTORS' MEETING

The meeting was called to order at 7:00 p.m. on September 26, 2005. All members of the board were present.

Page: 1 of 1   Words: 132   Insert

TIP

What happens if I click the Distinguish style source option below the Reveal Formatting task pane?

When you click this option (☐ changes to ☑), Word changes the appearance of the Reveal Formatting task pane to include the names of any styles used in your document. For more information on using styles, see the section "Apply Formatting Using Styles."

Options

☑ Distinguish style source

☐ Show all formatting marks

Compare Formatting

You can compare the formatting of one selection to another and have Word update one of the selections so that it matches the other. This feature is useful for ensuring that you apply consistent manual formatting to multiple selections.

① Select the text containing the formatting that you want to compare.

② Click the **Home** tab.

③ Click the **Styles** 🔲.

The Styles task pane appears.

④ Click the **Style Inspector** icon (🔁).

The Style Inspector pane appears.

⑤ Click 🔍.

● The Reveal Formatting pane appears.

⑥ Click ✕ to close the Styles pane and the Style Inspector pane.

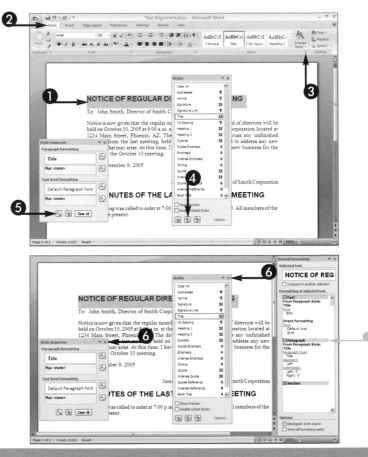

⑦ Click the **Compare to another selection** option (☐ changes to ☑).

⑧ Select the text that you want to compare to the text you selected in Step **1**.

● The two selections appear here.

● Formatting differences between the selections appear here.

⑨ To match the formatting of the selections, position the mouse pointer so that ☑ appears.

⑩ Click ☑.

⑪ Click **Apply Formatting of Original Selection**.

Word applies the formatting of the first selection to the second selection.

⑫ Click anywhere to continue working.

● You can click ✕ to close the Reveal Formatting task pane.

NOTICE OF REGULAR DIRECTORS' MEETING

To: John Smith, Director of Smith Corporation

Notice is now given that the regular monthly meeting of the board of directors will be held on October 10, 2005 at 9:00 a.m. at the principal office of the corporation located at 1234 Main Street, Phoenix, AZ. The directors will meet to discuss any unfinished business from the last meeting, held on September 6, 2005 and to address any new business that may arise. At this time, I have received one item of new business for the agenda of the October 10 meeting.

Dated September 9, 2005

James O'Donnell, Secretary of Smith Corporation

MINUTES OF THE LAST DIRECTORS' MEETING

The meeting was called to order at 7:00 p.m. on September 26, 2005. All members of the board were present.

What kind of formatting differences does Word identify in the Reveal Formatting task pane?

For any two selections, Word identifies differences in font, paragraph style, alignment, outline level, spacing before and after the paragraphs, line and page breaks, and bullets and numbering. You can make changes to any of these formatting differences by following the steps in the section "Review and Change Formatting."

What happens if I click the Show all formatting marks option below the Reveal Formatting task pane?

When you click this option, Word displays formatting marks in your document that represent tabs, spaces, paragraphs, line breaks, and so on.

Apply Formatting Using Styles

You can quickly apply formatting and maintain formatting consistency by using styles to format text. Styles are predefined sets of formatting that can include font, paragraph, list, and border and shading information.

You can store styles you use frequently in the Quick Style Gallery, but you also can easily use styles not stored in the Quick Style Gallery.

Apply Formatting Using Styles

USING THE QUICK STYLE GALLERY

① Select the text to which you want to apply formatting.

② Click the **Home** tab.

③ Click here to view available Quick Styles.

④ Click the **More** icon.

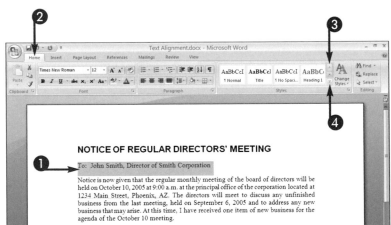

Word displays the Quick Styles Gallery.

● The style of the selected text appears here.

● As you position the mouse pointer over various styles, Live Preview shows you the way the selected text would look in each style.

⑤ Click a style to apply it to the selected text.

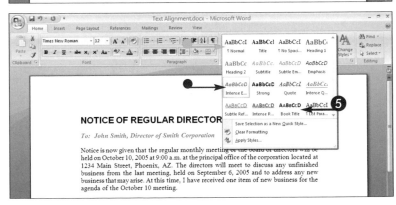

USING OTHER STYLES

1️⃣ Complete Steps **1** to **3** in the subsection "Using a Style from the Quick Style Gallery."

2️⃣ Click **Apply Styles**.

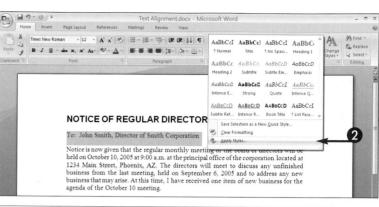

The Apply Styles pane appears.

3️⃣ Click here to open the Style Name list and then select a style.

Word applies the style to the selected text.

4️⃣ Click here to close the Apply Styles pane.

5️⃣ Click anywhere to continue working.

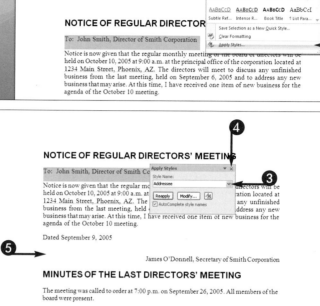

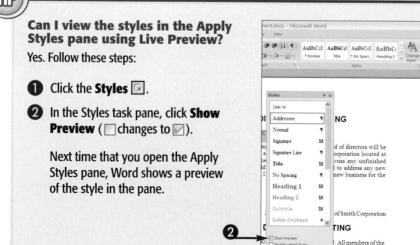

TIP

Can I view the styles in the Apply Styles pane using Live Preview?

Yes. Follow these steps:

1️⃣ Click the **Styles** 🔲.

2️⃣ In the Styles task pane, click **Show Preview** (☐ changes to ☑).

Next time that you open the Apply Styles pane, Word shows a preview of the style in the pane.

Switch Styles

You can easily change all text that is formatted in one style to another style. Using this technique can help you maintain formatting consistency in your documents.

Switch Styles

1 Place the insertion point in or select one example of text containing the formatting that you want to change.

2 Click the **Home** tab.

3 Click the **Styles** ⌐.

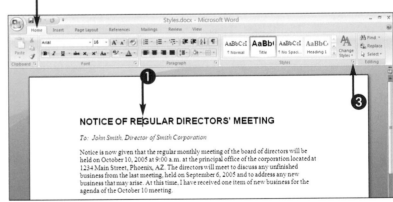

Word displays the Styles and Formatting task pane.

● The style for the selected text appears highlighted.

● Available styles appear here.

You can position ⌐ over any style to display its formatting information.

④ Position the mouse pointer here until 🔽 appears.

⑤ Click here to display a list of options.

⑥ Click **Select All Instance(s)**.

● Word selects all text in your document formatted using the style of the text you selected in Step **1**.

⑦ Click the style you want to apply to all selected text.

● Word changes all selected text to the style you selected in Step **7**.

⑧ Click anywhere to continue working.

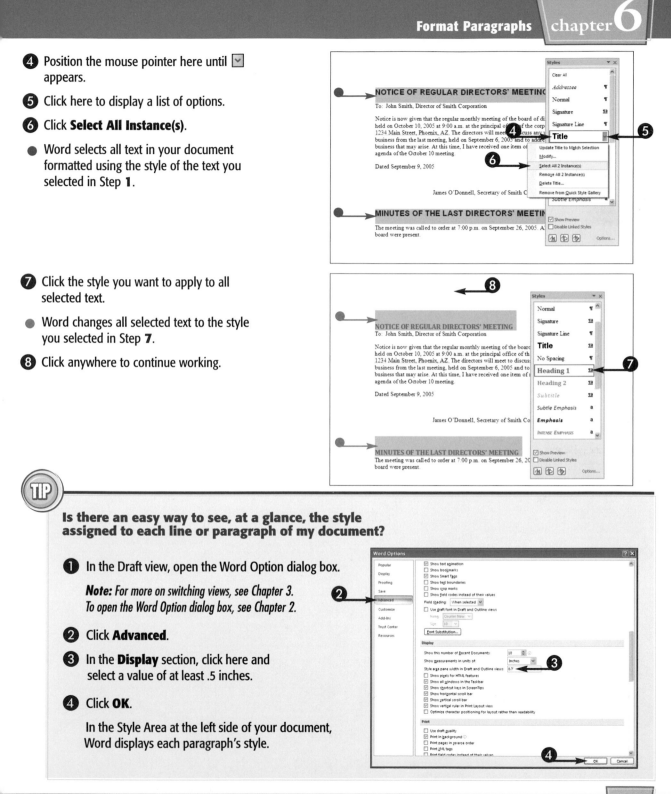

TIP

Is there an easy way to see, at a glance, the style assigned to each line or paragraph of my document?

① In the Draft view, open the Word Option dialog box.

Note: For more on switching views, see Chapter 3. To open the Word Option dialog box, see Chapter 2.

② Click **Advanced**.

③ In the **Display** section, click here and select a value of at least .5 inches.

④ Click **OK**.

In the Style Area at the left side of your document, Word displays each paragraph's style.

Save Formatting in a Style

You can easily create your own styles to store formatting information if you cannot find a built-in style that exactly suits your needs.

When you create a new style, you can make it appear in the Quick Styles Gallery.

① Format text in your document using the formatting you want to save.

② Select the text containing the formatting you want to save.

③ Click the **More** icon.

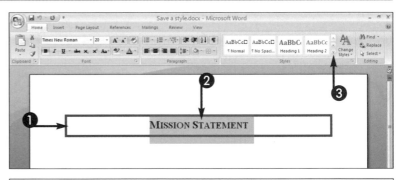

The Quick Style Gallery appears.

④ Click **Save Selection as New Quick Style.**

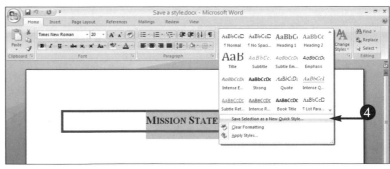

The Create New Style from Formatting dialog box appears.

5 Type a name for the style.

6 Click **Modify**.

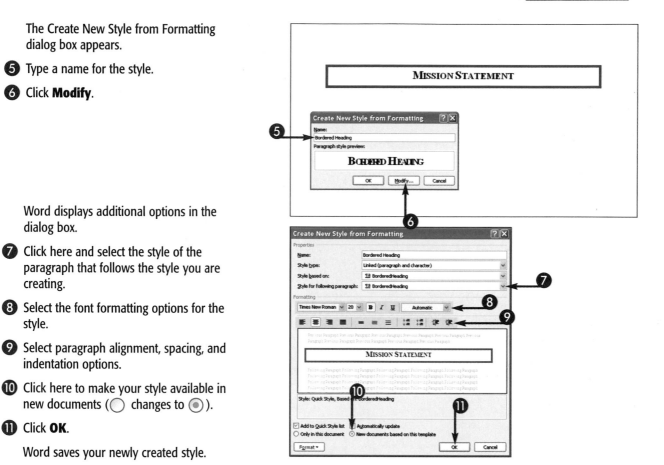

MISSION STATEMENT

Word displays additional options in the dialog box.

7 Click here and select the style of the paragraph that follows the style you are creating.

8 Select the font formatting options for the style.

9 Select paragraph alignment, spacing, and indentation options.

10 Click here to make your style available in new documents (⃝ changes to ⦿).

11 Click **OK**.

Word saves your newly created style.

TIPS

What happens if I click Format?

A menu appears that you can use to specify additional formatting. Select the type of formatting, and Word displays a dialog box where you can add more formatting characteristics to the style.

What does the Style based on option do?

Every style you create is based on a built-in Word style. Changing a built-in style can result in many styles changing. For example, many styles are based on the Normal style. If you change the font of the Normal style, you change the font of all styles based on the Normal style.

Modify a Style

At some point you may decide that the formatting of a style is close to but not exactly what you want. You do not need to create a new style; modify the existing one.

You can modify a style so that Word automatically updates the style's definition if you apply manual formatting to a paragraph using this style.

Modify a Style

① Open a document containing the style you want to change.

② Click the **Home** tab.

③ Click the **Styles** ▣ to display the Styles pane.

④ Position the mouse pointer over the style you want to change. ☑ appears.

⑤ Click here.

⑥ Click **Modify**.

The Modify Style dialog box appears.

⑦ Select any font formatting or paragraph formatting changes you want to make.

⑧ Click here (○ changes to ◉) to make the modified style available in new documents.

⑨ Click here (☐ changes to ☑) to add the style to the Quick Style Gallery.

⑩ Click **OK**.

Word updates all text in the document formatted with the style you changed.

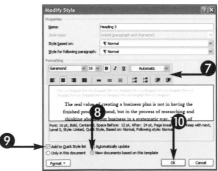

Add Paragraph Shading

Shading is another technique you can use to draw your reader's attention. Shading appears when you print your document; if you do not use a color printer, make sure you select a shade of gray for your shading.

Add Paragraph Shading

① Place the insertion point in the paragraph that you want to shade.

② Click the **Home** tab.

③ Click ▼ on the **Shading** icon (🖌️).

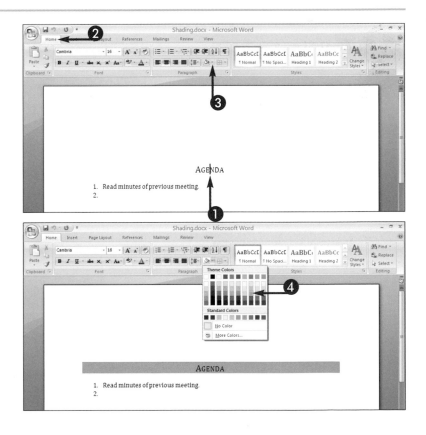

The Theme Colors gallery appears.

④ Point at a color.

Live Preview highlights the paragraph containing the insertion point with the color at which the mouse points.

⑤ Click a color to select it as the shading color for the paragraph.

Format Pages

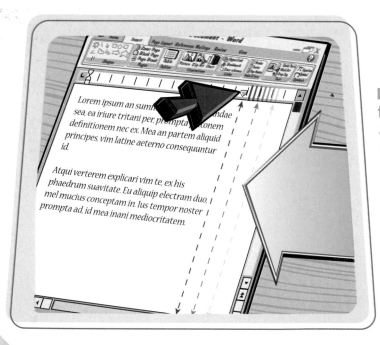

In addition to applying formatting to characters and paragraphs, you can apply formatting to pages of your Word document. Find out how to get your page to look its best in this chapter.

Adjust Margins

You can adjust the right, left, top, and bottom margins of your document. When you adjust margins, Word sets the margins for the entire document.

By default, Word sets all margins — left, right top, and bottom — to 1 inch.

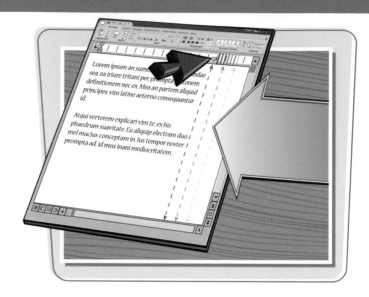

Adjust Margins

① Click anywhere in the document or section where you want to change margins.

② Click the **Page Layout** tab.

③ Click **Margins**.

The Margins Gallery appears.

If the margins you want to use appear in the Margins Gallery, click them and skip the rest of these steps; otherwise, proceed with Steps **4** to **9**.

④ Click **Custom Margins**.

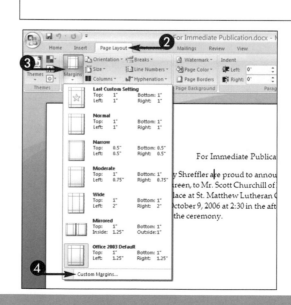

The Page Setup dialog box appears, displaying the Margins tab.

● The current margin settings appear here.

5 Drag the mouse pointer over any margin.

6 Type a new margin setting.

7 Repeat Steps **5** to **6** for each margin setting.

8 Click **OK**.

Word saves your changes.

TIPS

Can I change the margins for just one part of my document?

Yes, you can if you divide your document into sections using section breaks. You can set distinct margins for each section of a document. See the section "Insert a Section Break" for more information.

Can I use the mouse to change margins?

Yes. In Print Layout view, margins appear blue on the ruler. Move the mouse into the ruler area, between the white and blue portions of the ruler. ⬚ changes to ↔ or ↕. Drag ↔ or ↕ to reposition the margin.

Insert a Page Break

You can insert a page break to force Word to start text on a new page. Word automatically starts a new page when the current page becomes filled with text.

You can insert a page break using either the mouse or the keyboard.

Insert a Page Break

USING THE MOUSE

① Position the insertion point immediately before the text that you want to appear on a new page.

② Click the **Insert** tab.

③ Click **Page Break**.

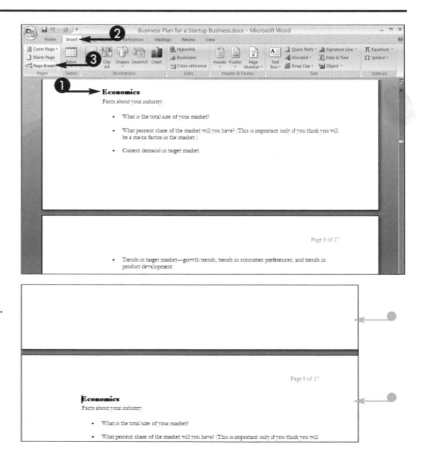

● Word inserts a page break and moves all text after the page break onto a new page.

USING THE KEYBOARD

1. Position the insertion point immediately before the text that you want to appear on a new page.

2. Press **Ctrl** + **Enter**.

Economics

Facts about your industry:

- What is the total size of your market?
- What percent share of the market will you have? (This is important only if you think you will be a major factor in the market.)
- Current demand in target market.

- Trends in target market—growth trends, trends in consumer preferences, and trends in product development.

● Word inserts a page break and moves all text after the page break onto a new page.

Economics

Facts about your industry:

- What is the total size of your market?
- What percent share of the market will you have? (This is important only if you think you will

---

TIP

Can I delete a page break?

You can delete page breaks that you insert into your document; you cannot delete page breaks that Word inserts when a page fills with text. Page breaks are easiest to see and delete in Draft view.

1. Click the **Draft view** icon (▭).

   Lines representing page breaks appear.

   Note: Lines without "Page Break" in them are page breaks inserted automatically by Word.

2. Click a page break line.

3. Press **Delete**.

In your marketing plan, be as specific as possible; give statistics, numbers, and sources. The marketing plan will be the basis, later on, of the all-important sales projection.¶

————————Page Break————————¶

Economics¶

Facts about your industry:¶

- → What is the total size of your market?¶
- → What percent share of the market will you have? (This is important only if you think you will be a major factor in the market.)¶
- → Current demand in target market.¶
- → Trends in target market—growth trends, trends in consumer preferences, and trends in product development.¶
- → Growth potential and opportunity for a business of your size.¶
- → What barriers to entry do you face in entering this market with your new company? Some typical barriers are:¶
  - → High capital costs¶
  - → High production costs¶
  - → High marketing costs¶

Words: 5,247   Insert

Control Text Flow and Pagination

You can control the placement of the automatic page breaks that Word inserts when you fill a page with text.

You can eliminate widows and orphans, keep an entire paragraph on one page, keep one paragraph with the next paragraph on a page, or insert a page break before a paragraph.

Control Text Flow and Pagination

① Select the text whose flow you want to affect.

Note: *To control widows and orphans, you do not need to select any text.*

② Click the **Page Layout** tab.

③ Click the **Paragraph** dialog box launcher icon (▣).

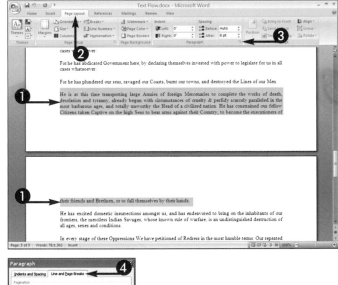

The Paragraph dialog box appears.

④ Click the **Line and Page Breaks** tab.

● This area contains the options you can use to control text flow and automatic pagination.

5 Click an option (☐ changes to ☑).

6 Repeat Step **5** as needed.

7 Click **OK**.

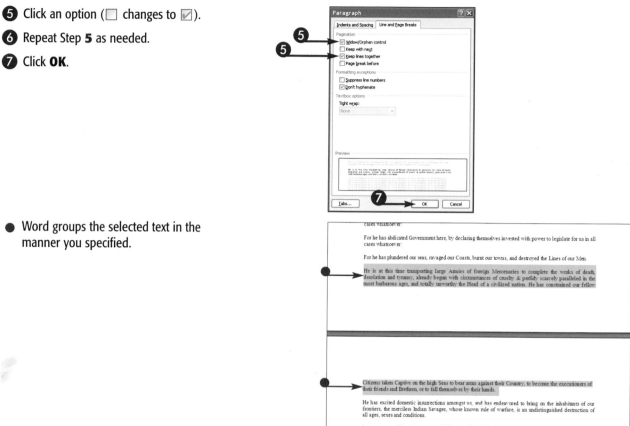

● Word groups the selected text in the manner you specified.

What is a widow?
Widow is the term used to describe when the first line of a paragraph appears at the bottom of a page and subsequent lines appear on the following page. Widows are distracting to reading comprehension.

What is an orphan?
Orphan is the term used to describe when the last line of a paragraph appears at the top of a new page and all preceding lines appear at the bottom of the previous page. Like widows, orphans are distracting to reading comprehension.

Align Text Vertically on the Page

You can align text between the top and bottom margins of a page if the text does not fill the page. For example, centering text vertically often improves the appearance of short business letters or report cover pages.

By default, Word applies vertical alignment to your entire document, but you can limit the alignment if you divide the document into sections. See the section "Insert a Section Break" for more information.

Align Text Vertically on the Page

① In the document you want to align, click the **Page Layout** tab.

② Click the **Page Setup** ▣.

The Page Setup dialog box appears.

③ Click the **Layout** tab.

④ Click the **Vertical alignment** ▾ and select a vertical alignment choice.

● To align all pages from the insertion point to the end of the document, click the **Apply to** ▾ and select **This point forward**.

⑤ Click **OK**.

● Word applies vertical alignment.

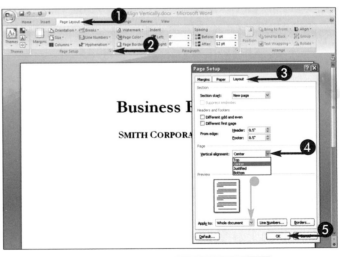

Business Plan

SMITH CORPORATION

Change Page Orientation

You can change the direction that text prints from the standard portrait orientation of 8½ inches x 11 inches to landscape orientation of 11 inches x 8½ inches.

To remember the difference between the orientations, think of paintings. Leonardo da Vinci painted his famous Mona Lisa portrait with the canvas oriented vertically. Georges Seurat painted his famous Sunday Afternoon on the Island of La Grande Jatte landscape with the canvas oriented horizontally.

Change Page Orientation

① Click anywhere in the document.

Note: *The document in this example appears zoomed out to show orientation changes more clearly.*

② Click the **Page Layout** tab.

③ Click **Orientation**.

● The current orientation appears highlighted.

④ Click an option.

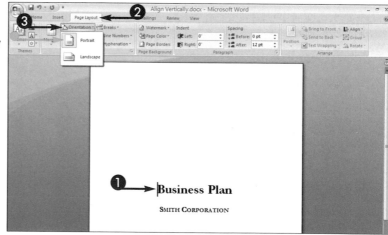

● Word changes the orientation.

Note: *By default, Word changes the orientation for the entire document. To limit orientation changes, divide the document into sections. See the section "Insert a Section Break."*

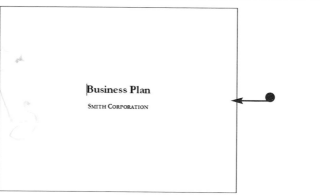

Insert a Section Break

You can insert a section break in a document to establish different margins, headers, footers, vertical page alignment, and other page formatting settings in different portions of your document.

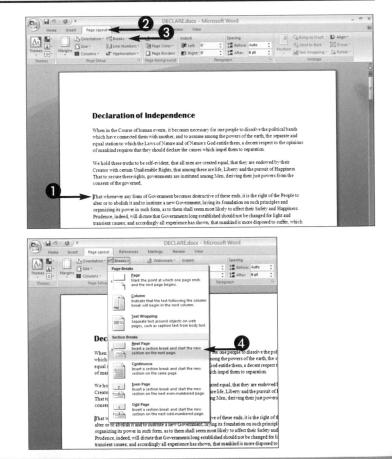

Insert a Section Break

1. Click in the location where you want to start a new section in your document.

2. Click the **Page Layout** tab.

3. Click **Breaks**.

The Break Gallery appears.

4. Click an option to select the type of section break you want to insert.

● Word inserts the type of break you selected.

❺ Click ▦ to display the document in Draft view.

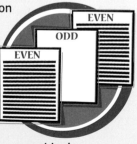

1 | Words: 1,362 | Insert ❺ 100%

● A section break line appears.

You can remove the section break by clicking the section break line and pressing the Delete key on your keyboard.

Declaration of Independence

When in the Course of human events, it becomes necessary for one people to dissolve the political bands which have connected them with another, and to assume among the powers of the earth, the separate and equal station to which the Laws of Nature and of Nature's God entitle them, a decent respect to the opinions of mankind requires that they should declare the causes which impel them to separation.

We hold these truths to be self-evident, that all men are created equal, that they are endowed by their Creator with certain Unalienable Rights, that among these are life, Liberty and the pursuit of Happiness. That to secure these rights, governments are instituted among Men, deriving their just powers from the consent of the governed,

————————————Section Break (Next Page)————————————

[That whenever any form of Government becomes destructive of these ends, it is the right of the People to alter or to abolish it and to institute a new Government, laying its foundation on such principles and organizing its power in such form, as to them shall seem most likely to affect their Safety and Happiness. Prudence, indeed, will dictate that Governments long established should not be changed for light and transient causes; and accordingly all experience has shown, that mankind is more disposed to suffer, which evils are sufferable, than to right themselves by abolishing the forms to which they are accustomed. But when a long train of abuses and usurpations, pursuing invariably the same Object evinces a design to reduce them under absolute Despotism, it is their right, it is their duty, to throw off such Government, and to provide new Guards for their future security.

Such has been the patient sufferance of these colonies; and such is now the necessity which constrains them to alter their former Systems of Government. The history of the present King of Great Britain is a history of repeated injuries and usurpations, all having in direct object the establishment of an absolute Tyranny over these States. To prove this, let Facts be submitted to a candid world.

Line: 1 | Words: 1,362 | Insert | 100%

 TIPS

How does Word handle printing when I insert a section break?

Section breaks are formatting marks that do not print; instead, the effects of the section break are apparent when you print. For example, if you insert a Next Page section break, Word starts the text that immediately follows the section break on a new page.

What happens if I select Even page or Odd page?

Word starts the next section of your document on the next even or odd page. If you insert an Even page section break on an odd page, Word leaves the odd page blank. Similarly, if you insert an Odd page section break on an even page, Word leaves the even page blank.

Add Page Numbers to a Document

You can have Word automatically print page numbers on the pages of your document. As you edit your document to add or remove text, Word adjusts the document and the page numbers accordingly.

Page numbers appear on-screen only in Print Layout view.

① Click the **Insert** tab.

② Click **Page Numbers**.

Page number placement options appear.

③ Click a placement option.

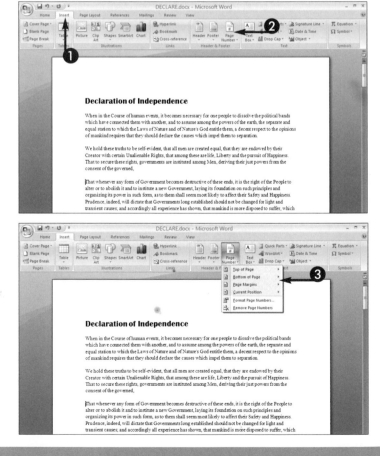

A gallery of page number alignment and formatting options appears.

④ Click an option.

The page number appears in the header or footer.

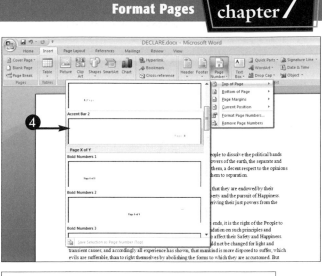

⑤ Click the **Print Layout** icon (▭) to display the document in Print Layout view and continue working on the document.

● The page number appears in the location and formatting you selected.

TIP

How can I start each section of my document with Page 1?

If your company's style calls for each chapter of a document to start on Page 1, you can break the document into sections and use these steps to start each section on Page 1.

① Place the insertion point in the first section of your document and complete Steps **1** to **4** in this section.

② Repeat Steps **1** to **3** in this section, selecting **Format Page Numbers** in Step **3**.

③ In the Page Numbering section, click **Start at** (○ changes to ◉) and type **1** in the box.

④ Click **OK**.

⑤ Repeat these steps for each subsequent section of your document.

Add Line Numbers to a Document

You can add numbers to the left edge of every line of your document. Line numbers are particularly useful for proofreading; proofreaders can refer to locations in the document by their line numbers.

Line numbers appear on-screen only in Print Layout view.

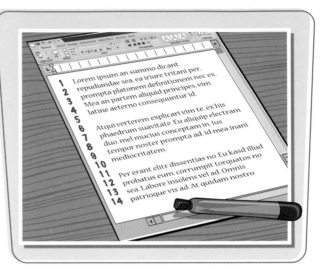

ADD LINE NUMBERS

① Click ▣ to display the document in Print Layout view.

② Click the **Page Layout** tab.

③ Click **Line Numbers**.

④ Click a line numbering option.

This example uses Continuous.

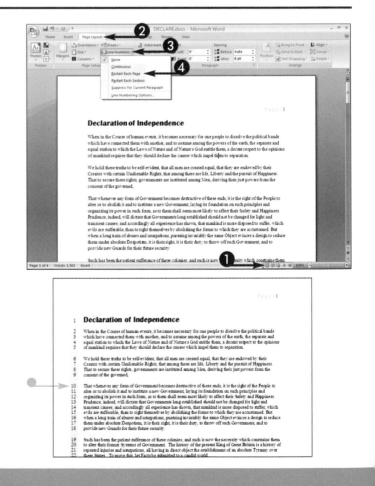

● Word assigns line numbers to each line of your document.

NUMBER IN UNUSUAL INCREMENTS

1 Complete Steps **1** to **3** in the subsection "Add Line Numbers" to add line numbers to your document.

2 Repeat Steps **1** to **3** in the subsection "Add Line Numbers," selecting **More Line Numbering** in Step **3**.

The Layout tab of the Page Setup dialog box appears.

3 Click **Line Numbers.**

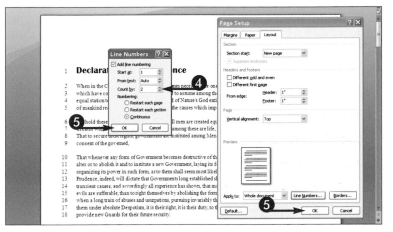

The Line Numbers dialog box appears.

4 Click the **Count by** ⬆ to specify an increment for line numbers.

For example, set **Count by** to 2 to number lines sequentially with even numbers.

5 Click **OK** twice.

Line numbers in the increment you selected appear on-screen.

TIPS

What does the From text option control in the Line Numbers dialog box?

Using this option, you can specify the position in inches in the left margin where line numbers will appear. Exercise caution, however; if you specify too large a distance, the line numbers will not appear or print.

How do I remove line numbers?

Follow Steps **1** to **4** in the subsection "Add Line Numbers," clicking **None** in Step **4**. Word removes line numbers from the document.

Using the Building Blocks Organizer

Building blocks are pre-formatted text and graphics that quickly and easily add a splash of elegance and pizzazz to your documents. Some building blocks appear by default as gallery options in Word.

Word organizes building blocks into different galleries, such as cover pages, headers, footers, tables, and text boxes, so that you can easily find something to suit your needs. The section adds a header building block to a document.

Using the Building Blocks Organizer

1 Open a document to which you want to add a building block.

Note: Depending on the type of building block you intend to use, you may need to position the insertion point where you want the building block to appear.

2 Click the **Insert** tab.

3 Click **Quick Parts**.

4 Click **Building Block Organizer**.

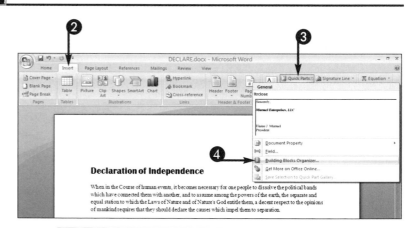

The Building Blocks Organizer window appears.

● Building blocks appear here.

● You can preview a building block here.

5 Click a column heading to sort building blocks by that heading.

Sorting by Gallery is most useful to find a building block for a specific purpose.

6 Click a building block.

7 Click **Insert**.

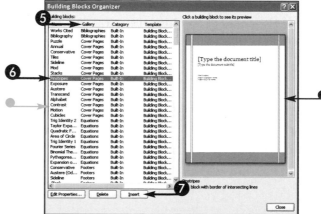

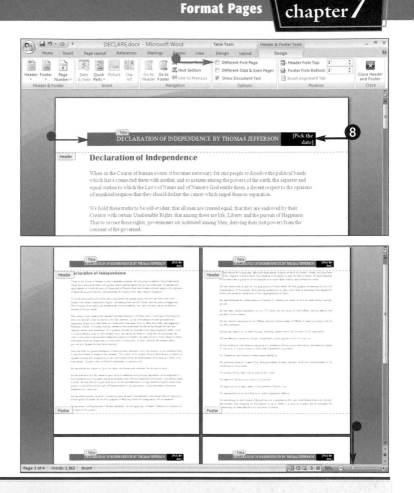

● The building block appears in your document.

8 Fill in any information required by the building block.

This example fills in header information.

● For headers and footers, you can make the building block appear on all pages of your document if you do not select **Different First Page**.

● You can zoom out to see multiple pages of your document and confirm the appearance of a header or footer on all pages.

TIP

How do I know where in my document Word will insert a building block?

Word places a building block in your document based on the building block's properties. Follow these steps:

1 Follow Steps **1** to **4** in this section to display the Building Blocks Organizer window.

2 Click **Edit Properties**.

The Modify Building Block dialog box appears.

3 Click the **Options** ☑ to determine where a particular building block will appear in your document.

Add a Header or Footer

You can use headers at the top of the page and footers at the bottom of the page to add information that you want to appear on each page of your document.

This section shows how to add a footer, but you can use the steps in this section to add a header by substituting "header" everywhere that "footer" appears.

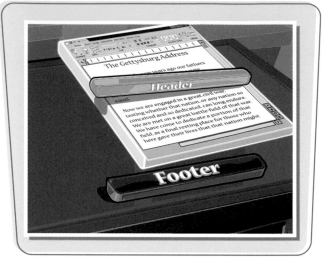

Add a Header or Footer

① Click the **Insert** tab.

② Click **Footer**.

The Footer Gallery appears.

③ Click a footer style.

Note: *The headers and footers that appear in the Header Gallery and the Footer Gallery are building blocks that also appear in the Building Blocks Organizer. See "Using the Building Blocks Organizer" for details.*

● The text in your document appears dimmed, and the insertion point appears in the Footer box.

● Header & Footer Tools appear on the Ribbon.

● Some footers contain information prompts.

④ Click or select an information prompt.

⑤ Type footer information.

⑥ Click **Close Header and Footer**.

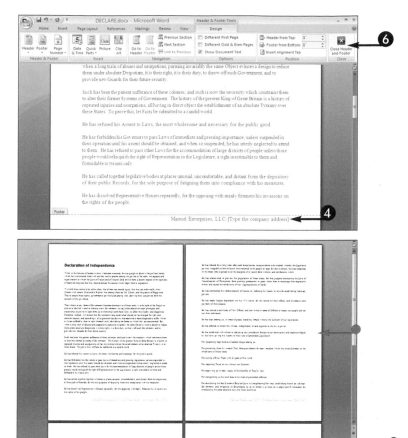

● Word saves your footer and redisplays your document text.

● You can zoom out to view the footer on multiple pages of your document.

Can I change the style of header or footer?

Yes. If you closed the header or footer pane, perform Steps **1** to **3**, clicking **Edit Header** or **Edit Footer** in Step **3**. Then, click **Header** or **Footer** at the left edit of the Ribbon to redisplay the Header Gallery or Footer Gallery and make a different selection.

Can I format text in a header or footer?

Yes. You can apply boldface, italics, underlining, and other character formatting the same way that you apply them in the body of a document. And, the Header area and the Footer area each contain two predefined tabs so that you can center or right-align text you type.

Using Different Headers or Footers Within a Document

You can use different headers or footers in different portions of your document. If you plan to use more than one header or footer, insert section breaks before you begin. See the section "Insert a Section Break" for details.

This section shows how to create different headers in your document, but you can use the steps to create different footers by substituting "footer" everywhere that "header" appears.

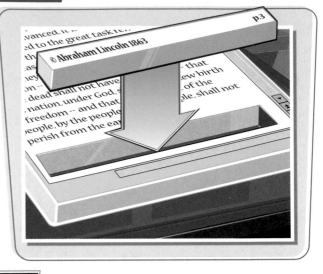

Using Different Headers or Footers Within a Document

① Click in the first section for which you want to create a header.

② Click the **Insert** tab.

③ Click **Header**.

The Header Gallery appears.

④ Click a header.

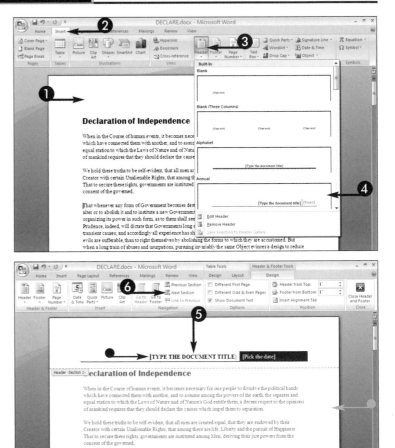

Word inserts the header.

● The text in your document appears dimmed.

● The insertion point appears in the Header- Section 1 box.

⑤ Type any necessary text.

⑥ Click **Next Section**.

● The Header-Section 2 box appears.

● Word identifies the header or footer as "Same as Previous."

⑦ Click **Link to Previous** to unlink the headers of the two sections.

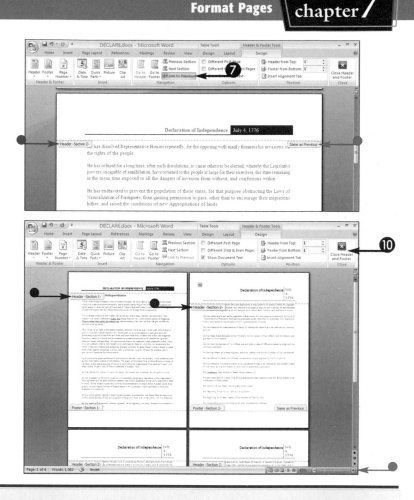

● Word removes the "Same as Previous" marking from the header.

⑧ Repeat Steps **2** to **4** to insert a new header in the second section; then repeat Step **5**.

⑨ Repeat Steps **6** to **8** for each section for which you want a different header.

● You can zoom out to preview the different headers.

⑩ Click **Close Header and Footer**.

TIP

Can I create different headers or footers for odd or even pages?
Yes, and you do not need to insert section breaks.

① Complete Steps **2** to **5** in this section.

② On the Design tab of the Header and Footer Tools, click **Different Odd & Even Pages.**

● Each header or footer box is renamed to Odd Page or Even Page.

③ Click **Next Section** to switch to the Even Page Header box or the Even Page Footer box and type text.

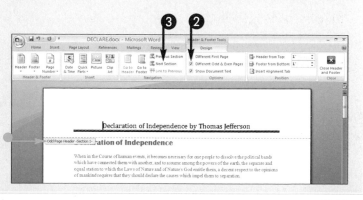

Add a Footnote

You can add footnotes to a document to provide additional explanatory information or to cite references to other works.

Footnotes are numbered 1, 2, 3, and appear within your document in Print Layout view and Full Screen Reading view. Footnote references appear in the body of your document in all views.

This text also available in Spanish.

Add a Footnote

① Click in the document where you want the footnote number to appear.

② Click the **References** tab.

③ Click **Insert Footnote**.

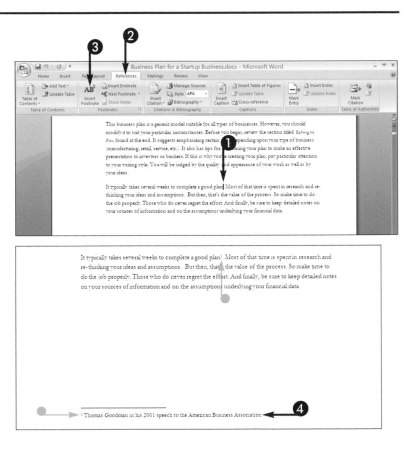

● Word displays the footnote number in the body of the document and in the note.

④ Type the text for the footnote.

⑤ Press Shift + F5 .

Word returns the insertion point to the place in your document where you inserted the footnote.

Add an Endnote

You can add endnotes to a document to provide additional explanatory information or to cite references to other works.

Endnotes are numbered i, ii, iii, and appear at the end of your document in Print Layout view and Full Screen Reading view. Endnote references appear in the body of your document in all views.

Add an Endnote

① Click in the document where you want the endnote number to appear.

② Click the **References** tab.

③ Click **Insert Endnote**.

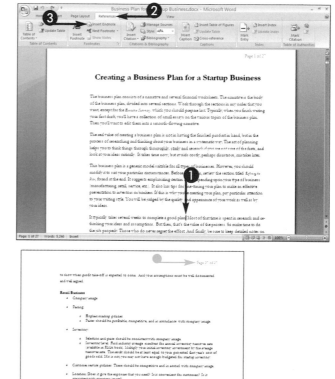

Word inserts the endnote number in the body of your document and at the end of your document.

● The insertion point appears at the end of your document in the endnote area.

④ Type the text for the endnote.

⑤ Press Shift + F5 .

Word returns the insertion point to the place in your document where you inserted the endnote.

View, Edit, or Delete Footnotes or Endnotes

Working in any view, you can view footnote or endnote text, modify the text, or delete the footnote or endnote.

VIEW FOOTNOTES OR ENDNOTES

1 Position the mouse I over the footnote or endnote number in your document (I changes to ⌑).

● A ScreenTip appears, displaying the footnote or endnote text.

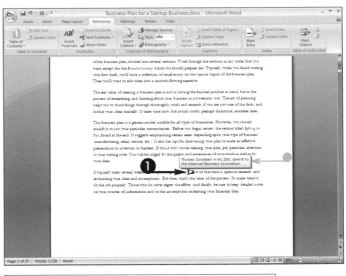

EDIT FOOTNOTES OR ENDNOTES

1 Double-click a footnote or endnote reference number in your document.

Note: To easily edit endnotes, press **Ctrl** + **End** to move the insertion point to the end of the document.

● In Print Layout view, Word moves the insertion point into the footnote or endnote.

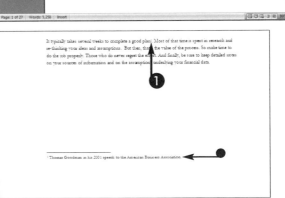

● In Draft view, Word displays footnotes in the Footnotes pane.

② Edit the text of the note as needed.

③ In Draft view, click the **Close** icon (☒) when you finish editing.

DELETE A FOOTNOTE OR ENDNOTE

① Select the reference number of the footnote or endnote you want to delete.

② Press **Delete** on your keyboard.

Word removes the footnote or endnote number and related information from the document and automatically renumbers subsequent footnotes or endnotes.

TIP

Can I print endnotes on a separate page?
To add your own custom list to AutoFill's list library, first create the custom list in your worksheet cells. Then follow these steps:

① Click in your document immediately before the first endnote.

② Click the **Insert** tab.

③ Click **Page Break**.

Word inserts a page break immediately before the endnotes, placing them on a separate page at the end of your document.

Convert Footnotes to Endnotes

If you change your mind and want to use endnotes instead of footnotes or footnotes instead of endnotes, you can convert one to the other.

Convert Footnotes to Endnotes

① Click the **References** tab.

② Click the **Footnotes** 🔲.

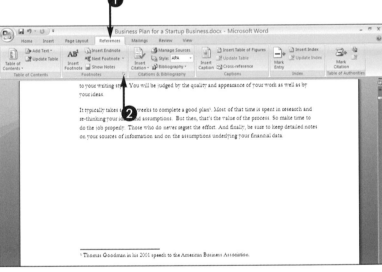

The Footnote and Endnote dialog box appears.

③ Click **Convert**.

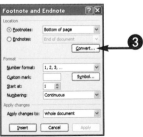

The Convert Notes dialog box appears.

④ Click the option that describes what you want to do (○ changes to ⊙).

⑤ Click **OK** to redisplay the Footnote and Endnote dialog box.

In the Footnote and Endnote dialog box, **Cancel** changes to **Close**.

⑥ Click **Close**.

● Word makes the conversion and renumbers footnotes and endnotes appropriately.

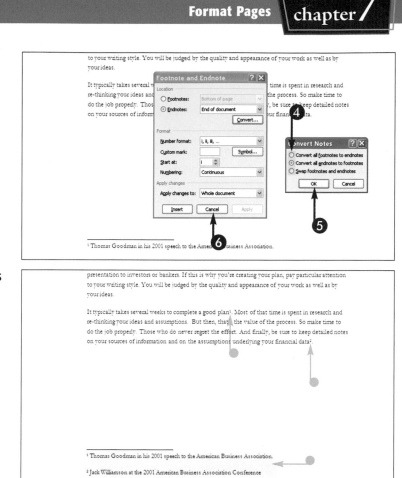

TIP

Is there an easy way to move the insertion point through the document from note to note?

Yes. Click 🔽 beside **Next Footnote** on the Ribbon. You can use these commands to scroll forward and backward through the document from endnote to endnote or footnote to footnote.

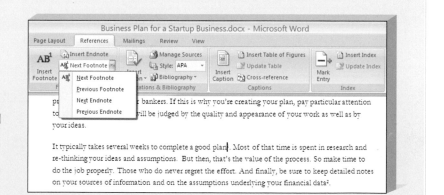

Generate a Table of Contents

You can automatically create a table of contents that updates as you update your document. Table of contents entries can come from text styled as Heading 1, Heading 2, and Heading 3 or from text you mark to appear in the table of contents.

You can create a table of contents at any time, continue working, and update the table of contents automatically with new information whenever you want. This section shows a table of contents created using heading styles.

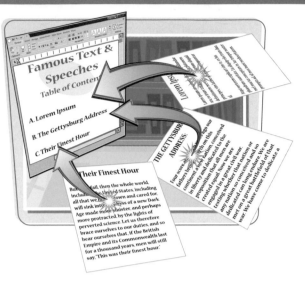

Generate a Table of Contents

INSERT A TABLE OF CONTENTS

① Press **Ctrl** + **A** to place the insertion point at the top of your document.

② Click the **References** tab.

③ Click **Table of Contents**.

The Table of Contents gallery appears.

④ Click a table of contents layout.

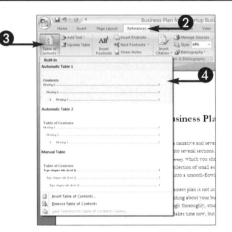

Word inserts a table of contents preceding the location of the insertion point.

● You can click ▲ or press **Ctrl** + **Home** to scroll up and view the table of contents.

● The information in the table of contents comes from text to which Heading styles 1, 2, and 3 were applied.

You can continue working in your document, adding new text styled with heading styles.

Note: *Do not type directly in the table of contents; make corrections in the document.*

UPDATE THE TABLE OF CONTENTS

1 Add text styled with heading styles or remove heading styles from text in your document.

For this example, text was restyled as Normal to remove it from the table of contents.

2 Click the **References** tab.

3 Click anywhere in the table of contents.

4 Click **Update Table**.

● You can click the **Update Table** icon (🗐) at the top of the table of contents.

The Update Table of Contents dialog box appears.

5 Click **Update entire table** (○ changes to ◉).

6 Click **OK**.

Word updates the table of contents to reflect your changes.

TIP

Can I include additional heading styles, such as Heading 4, in the table of con

Yes. Simply follow these steps:

1 Complete Steps **2** to **4** in the subsection "Insert a Table of Contents," selecting **Insert Table of Contents** in Step **4** to display the Table of Contents dialog box.

2 Click the **Show levels** 🔼 to change the number of heading styles included in the table of contents.

3 Click **OK**.

Word prompts you to replace the current table of contents.

4 Click **Yes** to update the table of contents.

Add a Watermark

You can add a watermark, which is faint text that appears behind information in a document, to your document to add interest or convey a message.

Watermarks are visible in Print Layout view and when you print your document.

Add a Watermark

① Click  to display your document in Print Layout view.

② Click the **Page Layout** tab.

③ Click **Watermark**.

● If you see the watermark you want to use in the Watermark gallery, you can click it and skip the rest of the steps in this section.

④ Click **Custom Watermark**.

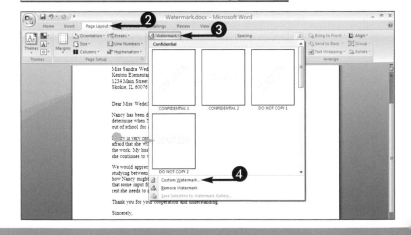

The Printed Watermark dialog box appears.

⑤ Click the **Text watermark** option
(○ changes to ●).

⑥ Click here and select the text to use as a
watermark or type your own text.

● You can use these options to control the
font, size, color, intensity, and layout of the
watermark.

⑦ Click **OK**.

● Word displays the watermark on each
page of your document.

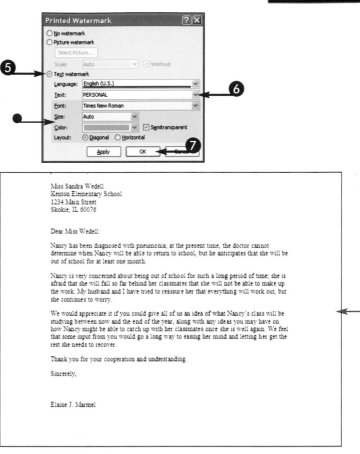

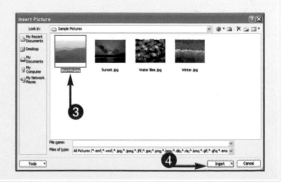

Add a Page Border

You can add a border around each page of your document to add interest to the document.

Add a Page Border

① Click 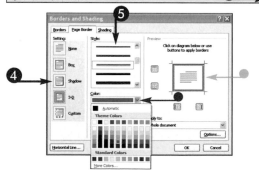 to display your document in Print Layout view.

② Click the **Page Layout** tab.

③ Click **Page Borders**.

The Borders and Shading dialog box appears, displaying the Page Border tab.

④ Click the type of border you want to add to your document.

⑤ Click a style for the border line.

● This area shows a preview of the border.

● You can click here to select a color for the border.

● You can click here to select a width for the border.

6 Click here to specify the pages on which the border should appear.

7 Click **OK**.

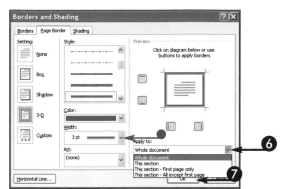

Word applies the border you specified.

Declaration of Independence

When in the Course of human events, it becomes necessary for one people to dissolve the political bands which have connected them with another, and to assume among the powers of the earth, the separate and equal station to which the Laws of Nature and of Nature's God entitle them, a decent respect to the opinions of mankind requires that they should declare the causes which impel them to separation.

We hold these truths to be self-evident, that all men are created equal, that they are endowed by their Creator with certain Unalienable Rights, that among these are life, Liberty and the pursuit of Happiness. That to secure these rights, governments are instituted among Men, deriving their just powers from the consent of the governed,

That whenever any form of Government becomes destructive of these ends, it is the right of the People to alter or to abolish it and to institute a new Government, laying its foundation on such principles and organizing its power in such form, as to them shall seem most likely to affect their Safety and Happiness. Prudence, indeed, will dictate that Governments long established should not be changed for light and transient causes; and accordingly all experience has shown, that mankind is more disposed to suffer, which evils are sufferable, than to right themselves by abolishing the forms to which they are accustomed. But when a long train of abuses and usurpations, pursuing invariably the same Object evinces a design to reduce them under absolute Despotism, it is their right, it is their duty, to throw off such Government, and to provide new Guards for their future security.

Such has been the patient sufferance of these colonies; and such is now the necessity which constrains them

TIP

Can I add a border that does not surround the page?

Yes. Follow these steps:

1 Follow Steps **1** to **6** to select the border you want to apply.

2 In the Preview area, click the border lines that you do not want to appear in your document.

3 Click **OK**.

Word applies the modified page border.

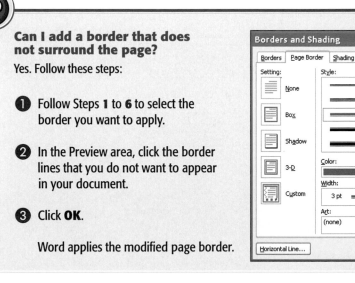

Create Newspaper Columns

You can format text in your document so that it appears in columns like the text in newspapers. Newspaper column formatting is useful when you are creating newsletters or brochures.

Text appears in newspaper columns only in Print Layout view.

Create Newspaper Columns

① Click ▣ to display your document in Print Layout view.

② Click the **Page Layout** tab.

③ Click **Columns**.

The Columns gallery appears.

Note: Although you can click a column layout and skip the rest of these steps, you can control your column layout better using the rest of these steps.

④ Click **More Columns**.

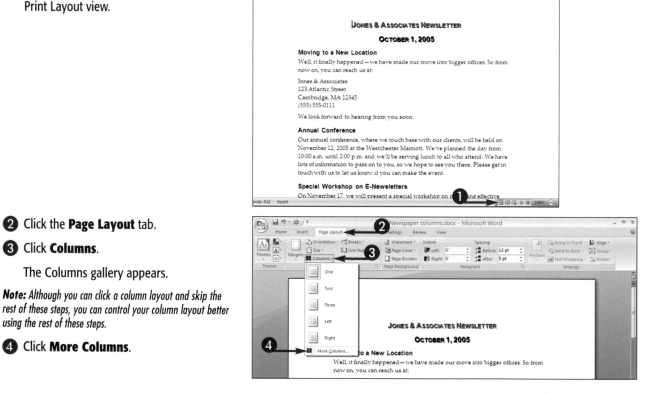

The Columns dialog box appears.

⑤ Click the kind of columns you want to create.

● You can use these settings to change the width of each column and the spacing between columns.

● You can click the **Line between** option (☐ changes to ☑) to add a line between columns.

● A preview appears here.

⑥ Click **OK**.

Word applies the column settings.

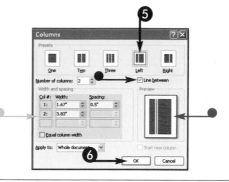

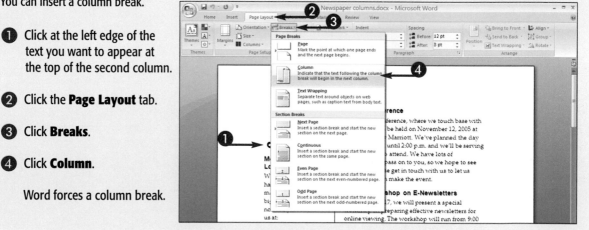

TIP

Can I force text from the left column to the top of the next column?
You can insert a column break.

① Click at the left edge of the text you want to appear at the top of the second column.

② Click the **Page Layout** tab.

③ Click **Breaks**.

④ Click **Column**.

Word forces a column break.

Print Documents

Now that your document looks the way you want it to look, you are ready to distribute it. In this chapter, you learn how to preview and print documents, print envelopes, and print labels.

You can preview your document before printing it to look for layout errors and other possible formatting inconsistencies.

Preview a Document Before Printing

1 Click the **Office** icon (🔘).

2 Position the mouse pointer over **Print**.

3 Click **Print Preview**.

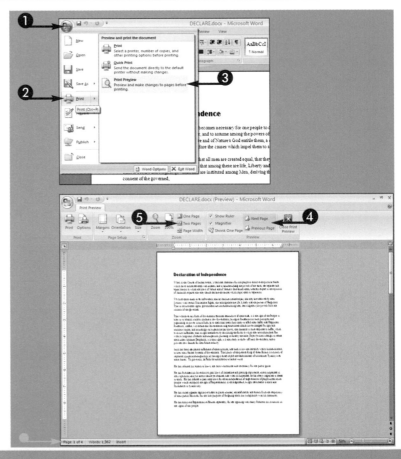

Your document appears in the Print Preview window.

● You can identify the page in your document using the Status bar.

4 Click **Next Page** or **Previous Page** to page through your document.

5 To view two pages at a time, click **Two Pages**.

Word displays two pages.

● You can click **One Page** to redisplay only one page.

⑥ To magnify an area of a page, position the mouse pointer over the area (⫽ changes to ⊕).

⑦ Click the area.

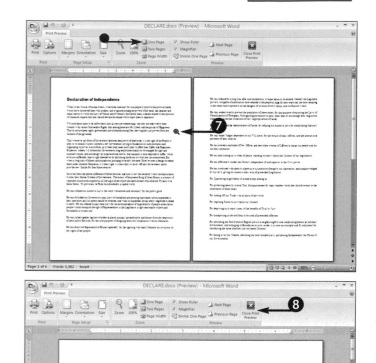

● Word magnifies the area.

⑧ Click **Close Print Preview** to close the Print Preview window.

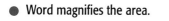

TIPS

What does the Shrink One Page button do?

When you click this button, Word shrinks the text of your document to one page less in size; a four page document becomes three pages and so forth. This feature is handy when your document fits on one page except for a few lines.

Can I edit my document while previewing it?

Magnify your document and then click the **Magnifier** option (☑ changes to ☐) and you can edit.

If your computer is connected to a printer that is turned on, you can print your document to produce a paper copy of it.

Jim,
Here is the quarterly report for my team. Sales jumped in the first part of the quarter. Mid-quarter sales were steady, while late quarter sales again jumped. The increase is due to the introduction of the two new lines of merchandise.

Print a Document

① Click 🔘.

② Position your mouse pointer over **Print**.

③ Click **Print**.

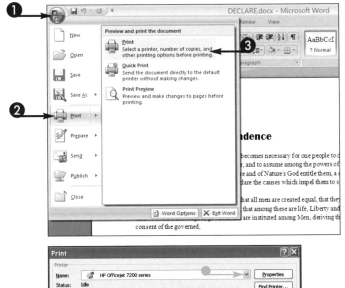

The Print dialog box appears.

● If you have more than one printer available, you can click here and select a printer.

④ Click a Page range option to identify the pages you want to print (○ changes to ◉).

5 To print more than one copy, type the number of copies to print here.

6 Click here and select what you want to print.

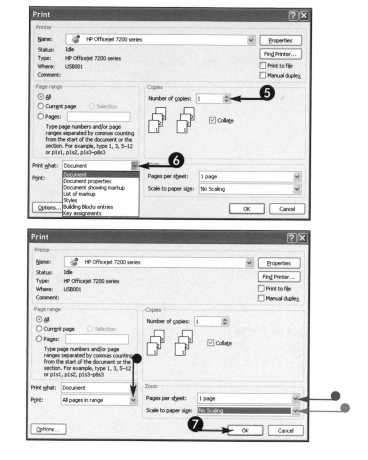

● You can click here to print odd or even pages instead of all pages.

● You can use this option to specify the number of pages you want to print on each sheet of paper.

● You can use this option to adjust the document to fit on a selected paper size.

7 Click **OK**.

Word prints your document using the options you selected.

TIPS

How can I print only certain text in my document?

Select the text before starting these steps. In Step **3**, click **Selection**, which is only available to you because you selected text.

Jim,
Here is the quarterly report for my team.

Sales jumped in the first part of the quarter. Mid-quarter sales were steady, while late quarter sales again jumped. The increase is due to the introduction of the two lines of merchan...

Can I print noncontiguous pages of my document?

Yes. Follow Steps **1** to **3**, clicking the **Pages** option (○ changes to ⊙) in Step **3**. In the Pages box, type the pages you want to print, such as **1,3,4,7-9**.

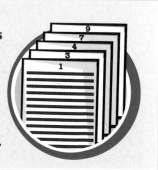

Change the Paper Size and Source

You can change the paper size on which you print your document and the paper source. For example, you may want to print on legal-sized paper that your printer stores in a separate paper tray.

Change the Paper Size and Source

1 Click the **Page Layout** tab.

2 Click the **Page Setup** dialog box launcher (⬚).

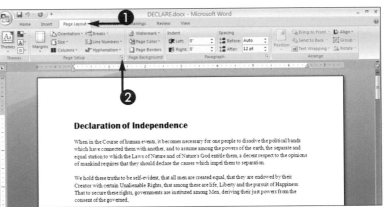

The Page Setup dialog box appears.

3 Click the **Paper** tab.

4 Click here and select the paper size you want to use.

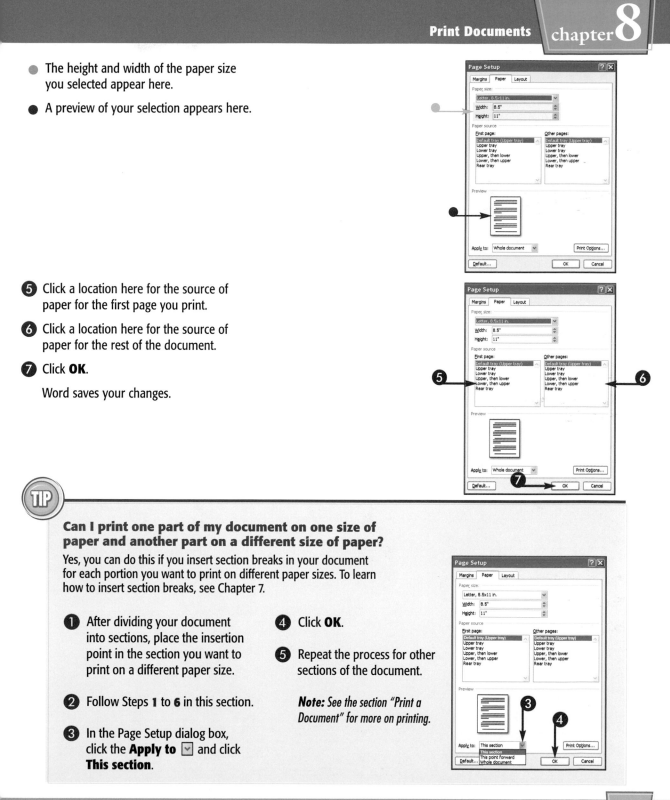

● The height and width of the paper size you selected appear here.

● A preview of your selection appears here.

⑤ Click a location here for the source of paper for the first page you print.

⑥ Click a location here for the source of paper for the rest of the document.

⑦ Click **OK**.

Word saves your changes.

TIP

Can I print one part of my document on one size of paper and another part on a different size of paper?

Yes, you can do this if you insert section breaks in your document for each portion you want to print on different paper sizes. To learn how to insert section breaks, see Chapter 7.

① After dividing your document into sections, place the insertion point in the section you want to print on a different paper size.

② Follow Steps **1** to **6** in this section.

③ In the Page Setup dialog box, click the **Apply to** ⊡ and click **This section**.

④ Click **OK**.

⑤ Repeat the process for other sections of the document.

Note: See the section "Print a Document" for more on printing.

Print an Envelope

If your printer supports printing envelopes, Word can print a delivery and return address on an envelope for you.

Consult your printer manual to determine if your printer supports printing envelopes.

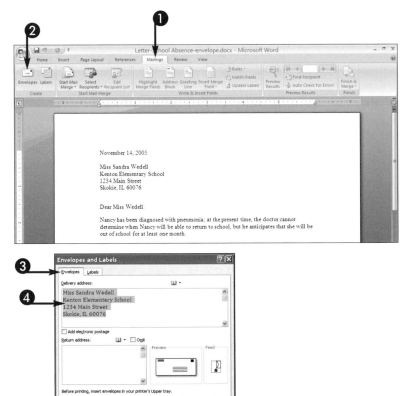

Print an Envelope

① Click the **Mailings** tab.

② Click **Envelopes**.

The Envelopes and Labels dialog box appears.

③ Click the **Envelopes** tab.

Note: *If Word finds an address near the top of your document, it enters that address in the Delivery address box.*

④ You can type a delivery address.

You can remove an existing address by pressing Delete on your keyboard.

By default, Word displays no return address in the Return address box.

5 Click here to type a return address.

6 Click **Print**.

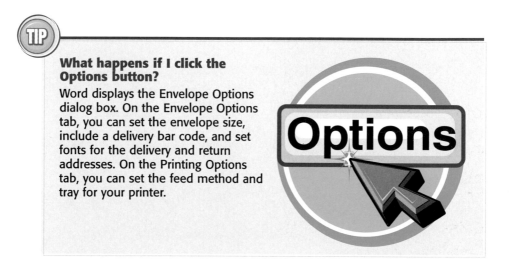

A dialog box appears if you supplied a return address.

Note: *If you save the return address, Word displays it each time you print an envelope.*

7 Click **Yes**.

Word saves the return address as the default return address and prints the envelope.

TIP

What happens if I click the Options button?
Word displays the Envelope Options dialog box. On the Envelope Options tab, you can set the envelope size, include a delivery bar code, and set fonts for the delivery and return addresses. On the Printing Options tab, you can set the feed method and tray for your printer.

You can format a Word document so that you can use it to type labels. For example, you can create address, name tag, and file folder labels.

This section demonstrates how to create a blank page of address labels onto which you can type address label information.

① Click the **Mailings** tab.

② Click **Labels**.

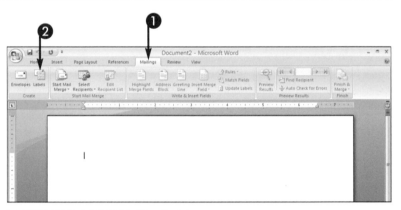

The Envelopes and Labels dialog box appears.

● This area shows the label currently selected.

③ Click **Options**.

The Label Options dialog box appears.

4 In this area, select the type of printer and printer tray to print labels (○ changes to ◉).

5 Click here to select the maker of your labels.

6 Click the product number of your labels.

7 Click **OK**.

8 Click **New Document** in the Envelopes and Labels dialog box.

Word displays a blank document, set up to hold label information.

9 Click the **Layout** tab.

10 Click **View Gridlines**.

11 Type a label.

12 Press **Tab** to move from label to label.

13 Repeat Steps **11** to **12** for each label you want to print.

14 Click 🔘 and click **Print**.

Word prints the labels.

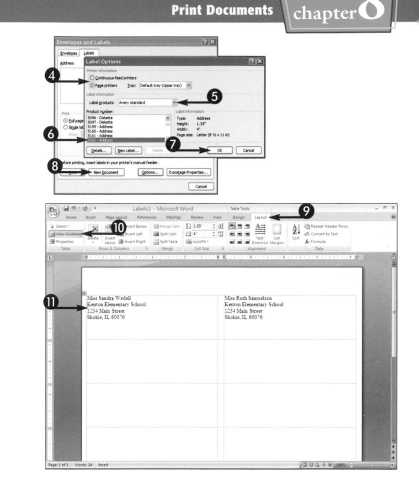

TIP

Can I print a single label?

1 Complete Steps **1** to **3** in this section to open the Envelopes and Labels dialog box.

2 Click the **Single label** option (○ changes to ◉).

3 Use these boxes to type the row and column of the label you want to use on the label sheet.

4 Type the label information here.

5 Click **Print**, and Word prints the single label.

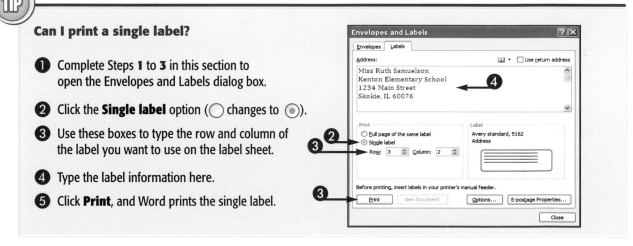

Create Tables and Charts

Do you want to keep the information in your Word document easy to read? The answer may very well be to add a table to contain your data. In this chapter, you learn how to create and work with tables in Word.

Create a Table

You can create a table and enter text into it. Tables are well suited to organize and display larges amounts of data.

The initial table you create may not contain the number of rows and columns you ultimately need, but you can always add rows or columns to your table later.

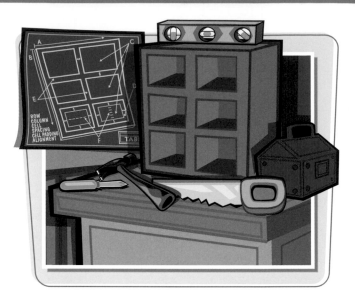

SET UP A TABLE

① Click in your document where you want the table to appear.

② Click the **Insert** tab.

③ Click **Table** to display a table grid.

④ Drag the mouse pointer across the squares that represent the number of rows and columns you want in your table.

● Live Preview draws a sample of the table on-screen.

⑤ Click the square representing the lower right corner of your table.

The table appears in your document.

● The insertion point appears in the table.

● Table Tools appear on the Ribbon, consisting of a Design tab and a Layout tab.

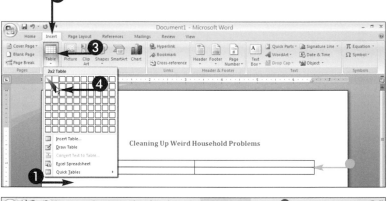

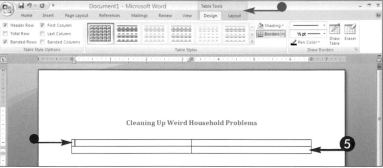

6 Click in the table cell where you want to enter information.

7 Type the information; if necessary, Word expands the row size to accommodate the text.

You can press **Tab** to move the insertion point to the next cell.

8 Repeat Steps **6** to **7** until you enter all of the table's text.

DELETE A TABLE

1 Click anywhere in the table you want to delete.

2 Click the **Layout** tab.

3 Click **Delete**.

4 Click **Delete Table**.

Word removes the table and its contents from your document.

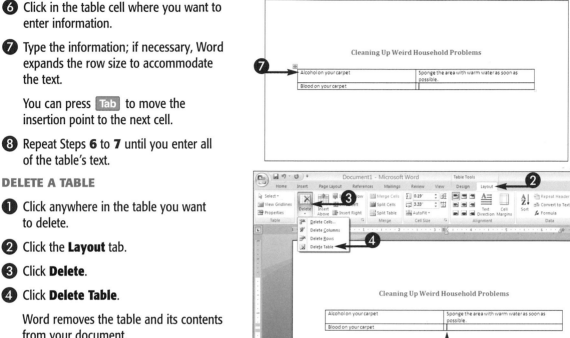

Can I add rows to the bottom of the table?

Yes, you can easily add rows to the bottom of a table by placing the insertion point in the last cell of the table and pressing the **Tab** key.

What, exactly, is a table cell?

A cell is the name of the square that appears at the intersection of a row and a column. In spreadsheet programs, columns are named with letters, rows are named with numbers, and a cell is named using the column letter and row number. For example, the cell at the intersection of Column A and Row 2 is called A2.

Change the Row Height or Column Width

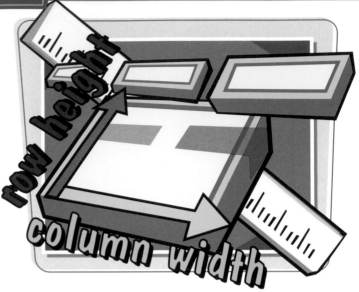

You can change the height of rows or the width of columns to accommodate your table information.

Make sure that you are working from Print Layout or Web Layout view; you can use the buttons on the status bar to switch views if necessary.

Change the Row Height or Column Width

CHANGE THE ROW HEIGHT

1 In either Print Layout or Web Layout view, position the mouse pointer over the bottom of the row (⌶ changes to ↕).

Note: For more on switching Document views, see Chapter 3.

2 Drag the row edge up to shorten or down to lengthen the row height.

● A dotted line marks the bottom of the row.

3 Release the mouse.

● The new row height appears.

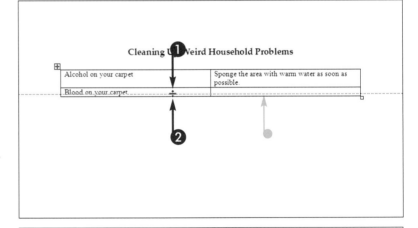

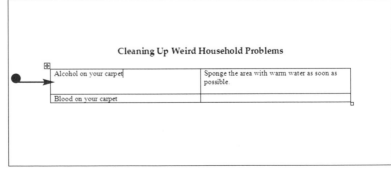

CHANGE THE COLUMN WIDTH

① Position the mouse pointer over the right side of the column ($\mathbb{I}$ changes to ↔).

② Drag the column edge right to widen or left to narrow the column width.

● A dotted line marks the side of the column.

③ Release the mouse.

● The new column width appears.

Note: When you change the width of any column except the rightmost column, the width of the column to its right also changes, but the overall table width remains constant. When you change the width of the rightmost column, you change the width of the entire table.

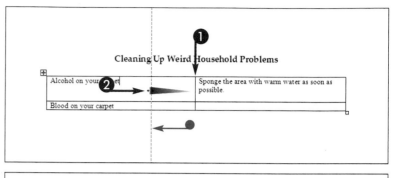

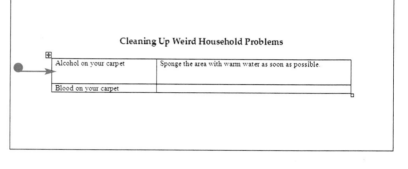

I tried to change the row height but the mouse pointer never changed to ↔. What did I do wrong?

You can change row height only when displaying your document in either Print Layout view or Web Layout view. Make sure you select one of those views by clicking the **Print Layout** icon ( ) or the **Web Layout** icon ( ). See Chapter 3 for more on understanding and switching between document views.

Can I easily make a column the size that accommodates the longest item in it?

Yes, you double-click the right edge of the column. Word widens or narrows the column based on the longest entry in the column. Word also adjusts the overall table size.

You can move a table to a different location in your document.

Make sure that you are working from Print Layout or Web Layout view; you can use the buttons on the status bar to switch views if necessary.

① In Print Layout or Web Layout view, position the mouse pointer over the table.

Note: For more on switching Document views, see Chapter 3.

● A handle (⊞) appears in the upper left corner of the table.

② Position the mouse pointer over the handle (⊞ changes to ✛).

③ Drag the table to a new location.

● A dashed line represents the table position.

④ Release the mouse button.

The table appears in the new location.

To copy the table, perform these steps but press Ctrl in Step **3**.

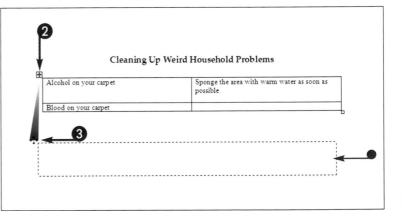

Resize a Table

If you find that your table dimensions do not suit your purpose, you can resize the table from Print Layout view or Web Layout view. For example, you may want to resize a table to make it longer and narrower.

Make sure that you are working from Print Layout or Web Layout view; you can use the buttons on the status bar to switch views if necessary.

Resize a Table

1 In Print Layout view, position the mouse pointer over the table.

Note: *For more on switching Document views, see Chapter 3.*

● A handle (□) appears in the lower right corner of the table.

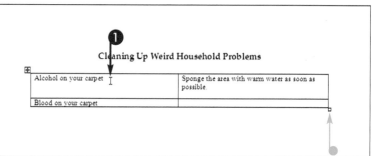

2 Position the mouse pointer over the handle (Ⅰ changes to ↘).

3 Drag the table up to make it smaller or down to make it larger (↘ changes to +).

Note: *You can also drag to the left or right as you drag up or down.*

● A dashed line represents the size of the table.

4 Release the mouse button.

The table's size changes.

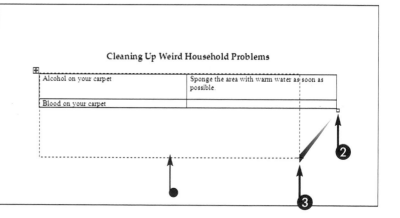

Add or Delete a Row

You can easily add rows to accommodate more information or remove rows of information you do not need.

ADD A ROW

1 Click in the row below where you want a new row to appear.

2 Click the **Layout** tab.

3 Click **Insert Above**.

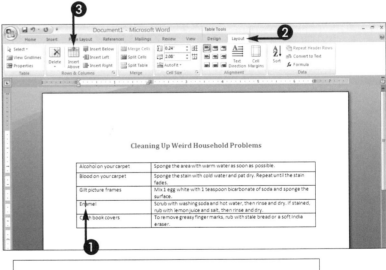

● Word inserts a row and selects it.

4 Click in the row to add information to the table.

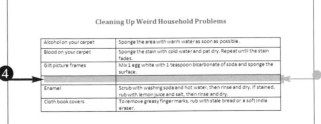

DELETE A ROW

① Click anywhere in the row you want to delete.

② Click the **Layout** tab.

③ Click **Delete**.

④ Click **Delete Rows**.

● Word removes the row and any text it contained from the table.

TIPS

Can I delete more than one row at a time?

Yes. Select the rows you want to delete before performing Steps **2** to **4** in the subsection "Delete a Row." To select the rows, position I outside the left side of the table (I changes to ⬦). Drag to select the rows you want to delete.

Can I insert more than one row at a time?

Yes. Select the number of rows you want to insert before you perform Steps **1** to **3** in the subsection "Add a Row." You can select rows below where you want the new rows and then perform Steps **1** to **3**, or you can select rows above where you want the new rows and, in Step **3**, click **Rows Below**.

Add or Delete a Column

You can add or delete columns to change the structure of a table to accommodate more or less information.

When you add columns, Word decreases the size of the other table columns to accommodate the new column but retains the overall size of the table.

ADD A COLUMN

1. Click in the column to the left of the column you want to add.

2. Click the **Layout** tab.

3. Click **Insert Right**.

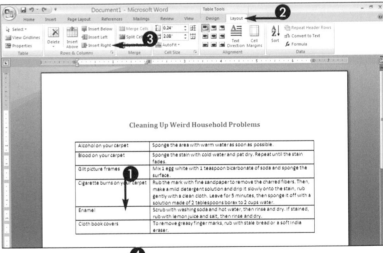

● Word inserts a column in the table to the right of the column you selected and selects the column.

4. Click in the column to add text to it.

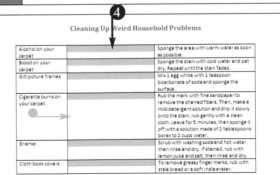

DELETE A COLUMN

① Click anywhere in the column you want to delete.

② Click the **Layout** tab.

③ Click **Delete**.

④ Click **Delete Columns**.

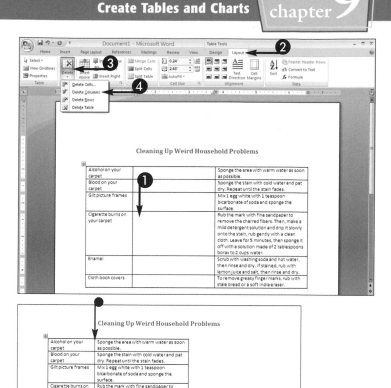

● Word removes the column and any text it contained from the table.

Word does not resize existing columns to use the space previously occupied by the deleted column.

TIP

Is there a way I can easily enlarge a table to fill up the space between the left and right margins after deleting a column?

Yes. Follow these steps:

① Click anywhere in the table.

② Click the **Layout** tab.

③ Click **AutoFit**.

④ Click **AutoFit Window**.

The table content and columns readjust to fill the space.

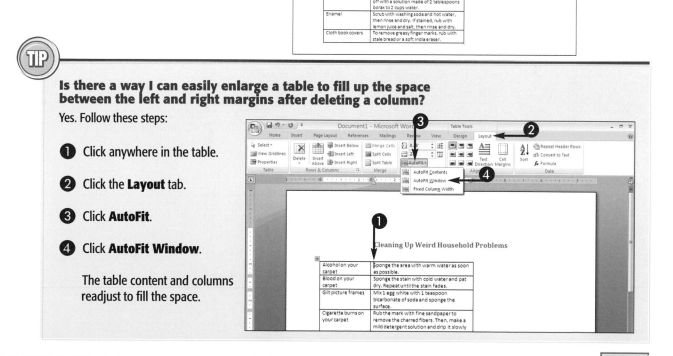

Set Cell Margins

You can set margins in table cells to make table information more legible.

Set Cell Margins

1. Click anywhere in the table.
2. Click the **Layout** tab.
3. Click **Cell Margins**.

   The Table Options dialog box appears.
4. Type margin settings here.
5. Click **OK**.

Word applies cell margin settings.

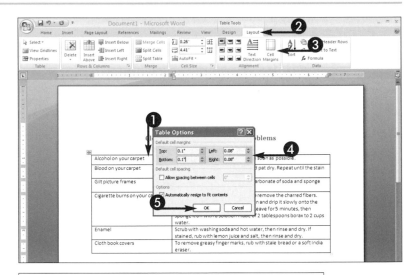

You can set spacing between table cells to make table information easier to read and more attractive.

1 Click anywhere in the table.

2 Click the **Layout** tab.

3 Click **Cell Margins**.

The Table Options dialog box appears.

4 Click here (☐ changes to ☑) and type a setting for space between cells.

5 Click **OK**.

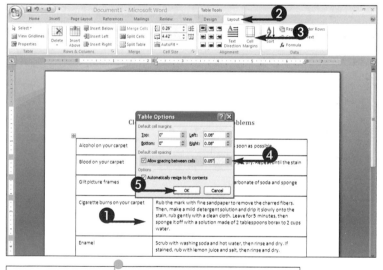

● Word adds space between cells.

Combine Cells

You can combine two or more cells to create one large cell, in which you can store, for example, a table title.

① Position the mouse pointer inside the left edge of the first cell you want to merge (I changes to ➚).

② Drag ➚ across the cells you want to merge to select them.

③ Click the **Layout** tab.

④ Click **Merge Cells**.

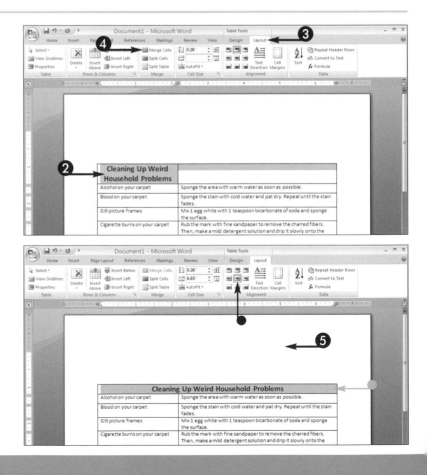

● Word combines the cells into one cell and selects that cell.

⑤ Click anywhere to cancel the selection.

● For a table title, you can click the **Align Center** icon (▤) to center text in the cell both horizontally and vertically.

Split Cells

If you find that you have more information in one cell than you want, you can split the cell into two or more cells that span one or more rows, columns, or both to make room for the extra information.

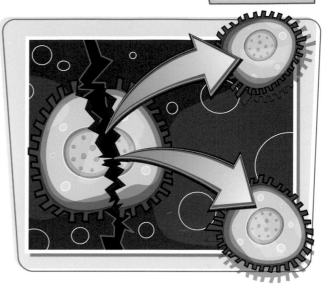

Split Cells

① Click anywhere in the cell you want to split.

② Click the **Layout** tab.

③ Click **Split Cells**.

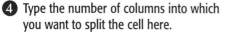

The Split Cells dialog box appears.

④ Type the number of columns into which you want to split the cell here.

⑤ Type the number of rows into which you want to split the cell here.

⑥ Click **OK**.

Word splits the cell.

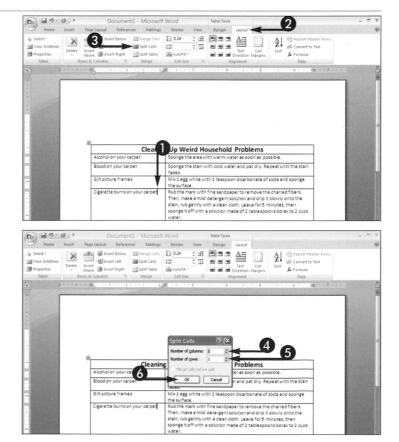

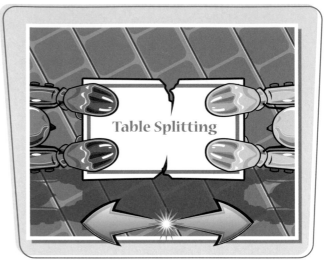

You can split one table into two tables. This feature is particularly useful if you discover that you should have created separate tables after you have entered a significant amount of information in one table.

① Position the insertion point anywhere in the row that should appear as the first row of the new table.

② Click the **Layout** tab.

③ Click **Split Table**.

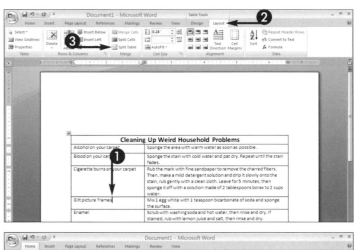

● Word separates the table into two tables and places the insertion point between the tables.

● Because the insertion point is not resting in a table cell, Table Tools no longer appears on the Ribbon.

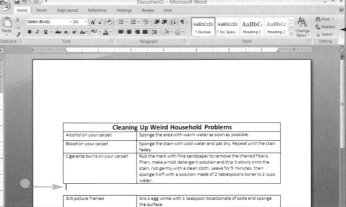

Add a Formula to a Table

You can place a formula in a cell and let Word automatically do the math for you. Word generally suggests the correct formula for the situation.

You can accept the suggested formula, as this example does, or you can select a different formula, as needed.

Add a Formula to a Table

① In a table containing numbers, click in a cell that should contain the sum of a row or a column.

② Click the **Layout** tab.

③ Click **Formula**.

The Formula dialog box appears, suggesting a formula.

● You can click here to select a number format.

● You can click here to select a different formula.

④ Click **OK**.

● Word places the formula in the cell containing the insertion point and displays the calculated result of the formula.

If you change any of the values in the row or column that the formula sums, you can click in the cell containing the formula and press **F9** to update the formula result.

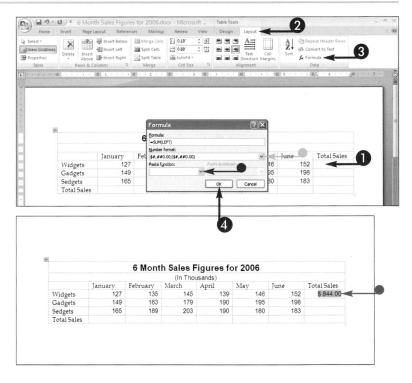

Align Text in Cells

To make your text look more uniform, you can align text or numbers with the top, bottom, left, right, or center of cells.

By default, Word aligns table entries at the top left edge of each cell.

Align Text in Cells

1 Click in the cell you want to align.

You can position the mouse pointer over the left edge of the cell whose alignment you want to change (I changes to ➚) and drag to select multiple cells.

2 Click the **Layout** tab.

3 Click an alignment icon.

● Word aligns the text accordingly in the cell.

4 Click anywhere to cancel the selection.

Add Shading to Cells

You can add shading to cells to call attention to them.

Add Shading to Cells

1 Click anywhere in the cell to which you want to add shading.

You can position the mouse pointer over the left edge of any cell (I changes to ➤) and drag to select multiple cells.

2 Click the **Design** tab.

3 Click **Shading**.

The Shading Gallery appears.

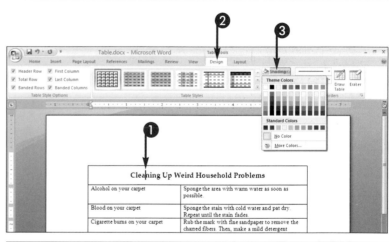

4 Position the mouse pointer over a color.

Live Preview displays a sample of the cell shaded in the proposed color.

5 Click a color.

● Word applies the shading to the selected cells.

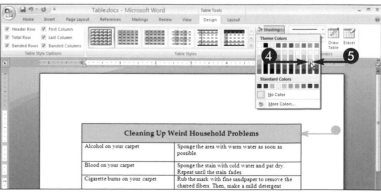

Change Cell Borders

You can change the appearance of cell borders to call attention to them.

1 Click in the cell you want to border.

You can position the mouse pointer over the left edge of any cell (I changes to $+$) and drag to select multiple cells.

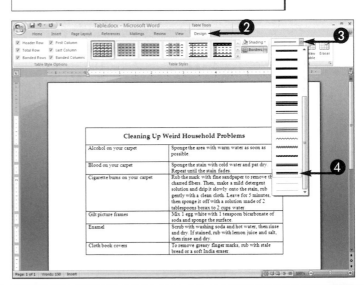

2 Click the **Design** tab.

3 Click **Line Style**.

The Line Style Gallery appears.

4 Click the line style you want to apply.

● You can click **Line Weight** and **Pen Color** to select the weight and color of the border line.

⑤ Click the **Borders** ▾.

The Borders Gallery appears.

⑥ Click the type of border to apply.

This example uses Outside Borders.

● Word applies the border using the selected line style, weight, and pen color to the selected cells.

⑦ Click anywhere to cancel the selection.

How can I remove borders from table cells?

Follow these steps:

① Complete Steps **1** to **3** in this section.

② Click the **Borders** ▾.

③ Click **No Border**.

Word removes the borders from the table cells.

On-screen, gridlines appear, but they do not print.

Format a Table

You can apply any number of predefined table styles to a table to format it.

① Click anywhere in the table.

② Click the **Design** tab.

③ Click the **More** icon.

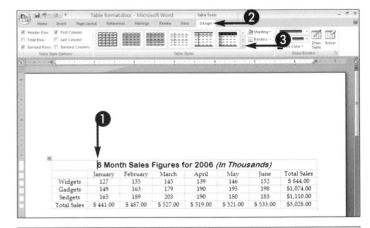

The Table Style Gallery appears.

④ Position the mouse pointer over a table style.

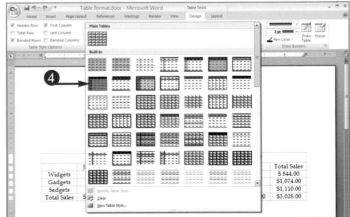

● Live Preview displays the table in the proposed table style.

❺ Repeat Step **4** until you find the table style you want to use.

❻ Click the table style you want to use.

● Word displays the table in the style you selected.

TIP

How can I remove a table formatting design?

You have several options:

● If you just applied the formatting, you can click the **Undo** icon (🔄).

● If you performed other actions since applying the table formatting design, perform Steps **1** to **3** in this section and then click **Clear**.

You can chart data from Microsoft
Office Word 2007. This process
uses Microsoft Office Excel 2007.

Add a Chart

① Click in the document where you want
a chart to appear.

② Click the **Insert** tab.

③ Click **Chart**.

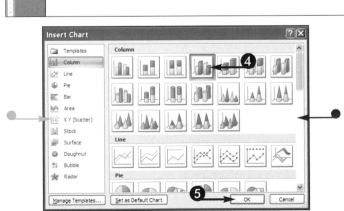

The Insert Chart window appears.

④ Click a chart type.

● Categories of chart types appear here.

● Chart types for each category appear here.

⑤ Click **OK**.

Microsoft Office Excel opens.

Word and Excel windows appear side by side on-screen.

● A sample chart of the data appears in Word.

● Sample data appears in Excel.

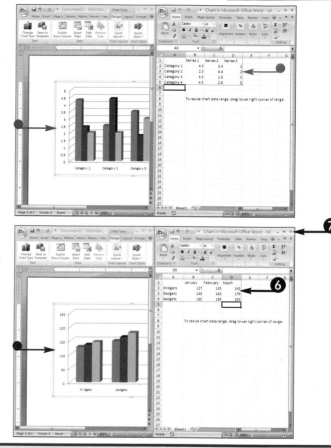

⑥ Change the data in Excel.

● The chart in Word updates to reflect the changes in Excel.

⑦ You can close Excel without saving by clicking the **Close** icon (☒).

TIP

Can I format the chart in Word?

Yes. When you maximize the Word window and select the chart, Word displays Chart Tools on the Ribbon. See Chapter 10 for more on WordArt and using drawing tools, which are very similar to chart tools.

● From the Design tab, you can select a layout and style from the Chart Layouts Gallery and the Chart Styles Gallery.

● From the Layout tab, you can set up chart and axes titles, add data labels, and modify the legend.

● The Format tab provides options for shape styles and WordArt styles.

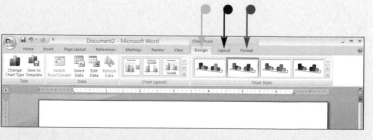

Chart Concepts

When creating a chart, you have a wide variety of choices. The type of chart you use depends on the information you are trying to convey to your reader.

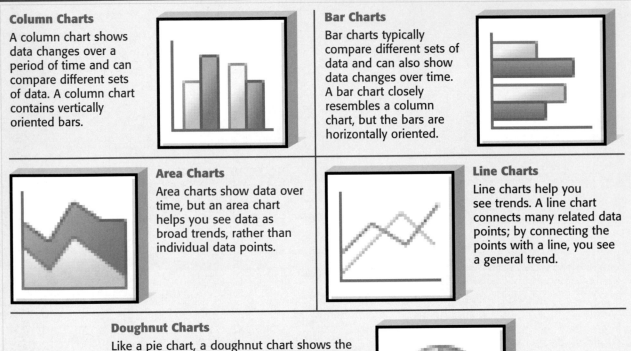

Column Charts

A column chart shows data changes over a period of time and can compare different sets of data. A column chart contains vertically oriented bars.

Bar Charts

Bar charts typically compare different sets of data and can also show data changes over time. A bar chart closely resembles a column chart, but the bars are horizontally oriented.

Area Charts

Area charts show data over time, but an area chart helps you see data as broad trends, rather than individual data points.

Line Charts

Line charts help you see trends. A line chart connects many related data points; by connecting the points with a line, you see a general trend.

Doughnut Charts

Like a pie chart, a doughnut chart shows the relationship of parts to a whole. Although a pie chart contains only one data series, a doughnut chart typically contains more than one data series. The doughnut chart is round like a pie chart, but each series in the doughnut chart appears as a separate ring in the circle.

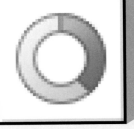

Pie Charts

Pie charts demonstrate the relationship of a part to the whole. Pie charts are effective when you are trying to show, for example, the percentage of total sales for which the Midwest region is responsible.

X Y Charts

Statisticians often use an XY chart, also called a scatter chart, to determine whether a correlation exists between two variables. Both axes on a scatter chart are numeric, and the axes can be linear or logarithmic.

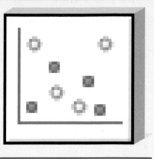

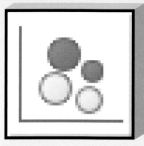

Bubble Charts

A bubble chart is a specific type of XY chart that compares sets of three values. The size of the bubble indicates the value of a third variable. You can arrange data for a bubble chart by placing the X values in one column and entering corresponding Y values and bubble sizes in the adjacent columns.

Stock Charts

Also called High-Low, Open-Close charts, stock charts are used for stock market reports. This chart type is very effective to display data that fluctuates over time.

Surface Charts

Topographic maps are surface charts, using colors and patterns to identify areas in the same range of values. A surface chart is useful when you want to find the best possible combination between two sets of data.

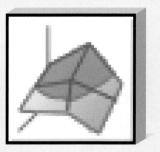

Radar Charts

You can use a radar chart to compare data series that consist of several different variables. Each data series on a radar chart has its own axis that "radiates" from the center of the chart — hence the name radar chart. A line connects each point in the series.

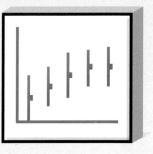

Work With Graphics

Although Word is primarily a word-processing software package, you can spruce up your documents using a variety of graphics, including WordArt, pictures, clip art, shapes, text boxes, and diagrams.

Add WordArt

WordArt is decorative text that you can add to a document as an eye-catching visual effect. You can create WordArt text as you create a WordArt graphic, or you can apply a WordArt style to existing text.

Add WordArt

1 Click the location where you want to add WordArt.

● You can select existing text and apply WordArt to it.

2 Click the **Insert** tab.

3 Click **WordArt**.

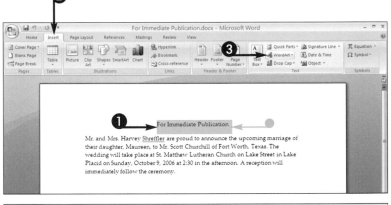

The WordArt Gallery appears.

4 Click the WordArt style you want to apply.

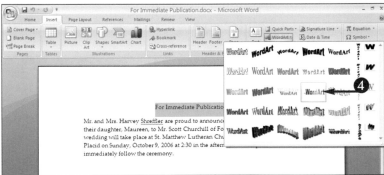

The Edit WordArt Text dialog box appears.

If you selected text in Step **1**, your text appears selected; otherwise, the words "Your Text Here" appear selected.

5 If necessary, type text.

● You can click ☑ to change the font or font size.

● You can click the **Bold** icon (**B**) or **Italicize** icon (**I**) to emphasize your text.

6 Click **OK**.

Word converts the text to a WordArt graphic and displays it, selected.

● Handles (■) surround the WordArt graphic.

● WordArt Tools appear on the Ribbon.

● You can click the **More** icon to open the WordArt Gallery and point at other WordArt styles to preview them; click one to change the WordArt style.

7 Click anywhere to continue working.

TIP

Can I delete the WordArt graphic or change the text?

1 Click the WordArt graphic.

● Handles (■) appear around the WordArt.

2 To change WordArt text, right-click the WordArt graphic and click **Edit Text**.

You can now edit the text.

You can press Delete to delete the WordArt.

Add a Picture

You can include a picture file graphic stored on your computer in a Word document.

Add a Picture

1 Click in your document where you want to add a picture.

2 Click the **Insert** tab.

3 Click **Picture**.

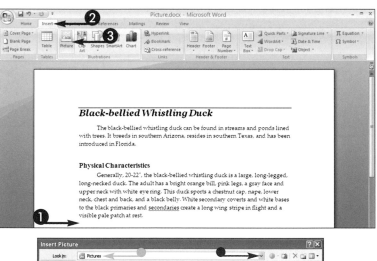

The Insert Picture dialog box appears.

● The folder you are viewing appears here.

● You can click here to navigate to a different folder.

● You can click these icons to navigate to commonly used locations where pictures may be stored.

④ Navigate to the folder containing the picture you want to add.

⑤ Click the picture you want to add to your document.

⑥ Click **Insert**.

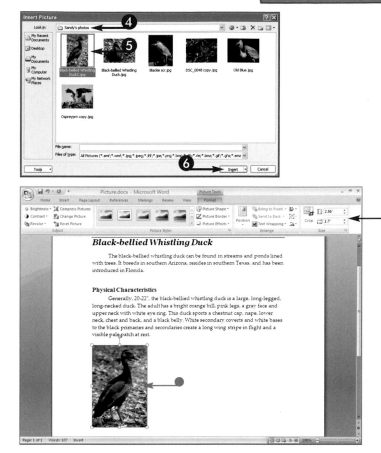

● The picture appears in your document, selected and surrounded by handles (▢ and ▢).

● Picture Tools appear in the Ribbon.

Note: To move or resize a picture, see the section "Move or Resize a Graphic."

Note: To control text wrapping, see the sections "Text Wrapping and Graphics" and "Wrap Text Around a Graphic."

You can delete the picture by pressing **Delete**.

TIP

How can I edit a picture?

① Click the picture that you want to edit or delete.

● Handles (▢ and ▢) surround the picture and Picture Tools appear in the Ribbon.

② Click a button on the Ribbon to make changes to the picture.

● For example, click **Contrast** to display the Contrast Gallery and increase the contrast in the picture.

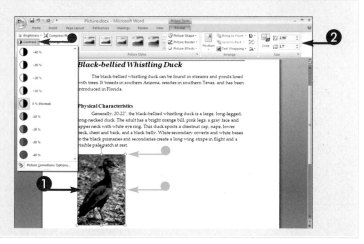

Add a Clip Art Image

You can add clip art images to your document to help get your message across and add graphic interest to your document.

You can locate images using the Microsoft Clip Organizer window or by searching for images.

Add a Clip Art Image

COPY IMAGES FROM THE CLIP ORGANIZER WINDOW

1. Click **Insert**.

2. Click **Clip Art**.

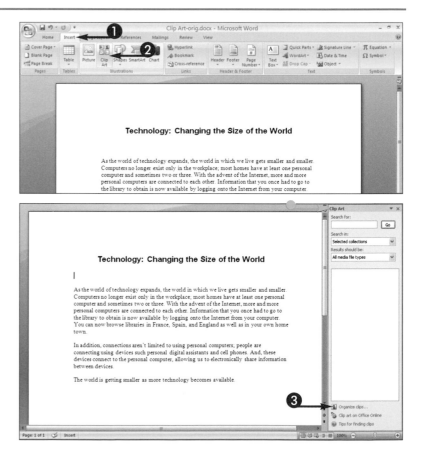

● The Clip Art task pane appears.

3. Click the **Organize clips** link.

*Note: The Add Clips to Organizer window appears when you have not cataloged picture, sound, and motion files on your hard disk. Click **Now** to catalog your media files.*

The Microsoft Clip Organizer window appears.

The Collection List displays folders containing clip art images.

A plus sign (⊞) beside a folder means that additional folders appear inside the folder.

④ Click ⊞ beside a folder to display the folders inside it (⊞ changes to ⊟).

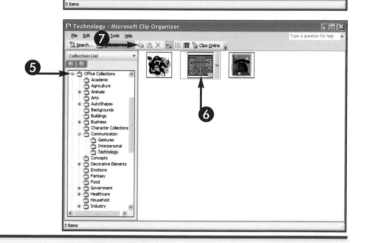

⑤ Click a folder or ⊞ beside the folder.

⑥ Click the image you want to add to your document.

⑦ Click the **Copy** icon (🖹).

Word copies the image to the Clipboard.

How can I copy more than one image to the Clipboard?
Follow these steps:

① In the Home tab, complete Steps **1** to **4** in this section, clicking your document on the Windows Taskbar.

② Click the **Clipboard** dialog box launcher icon (🔲).

③ Click **Microsoft Clip Organizer** on the Windows Taskbar.

④ Complete Steps **5** to **8** for each image you want available; then complete Steps **9** to **10**.

⑤ Click an image in the Office Clipboard pane to add it to your document.

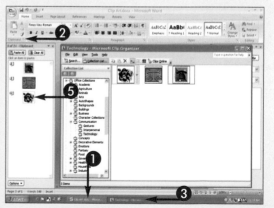

continued

You can copy an image you locate
using the Microsoft Clip Organizer
window to the Windows Clipboard
so that you can paste the image
into your document.

Add a Clip Art Image *(continued)*

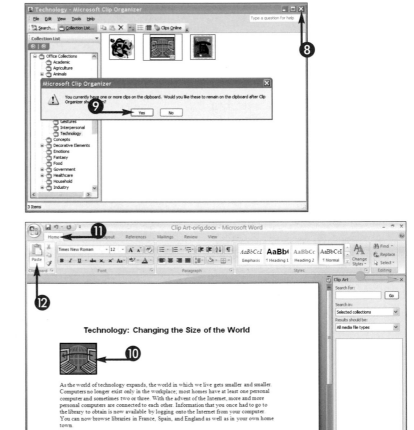

8 Click the **Close** icon (⊠) to close the
Microsoft Clip Organizer.

A message appears, asking if you want
to make the image you copied to the
Clipboard available after closing the
Microsoft Clip Organizer.

9 Click **Yes**.

Your document reappears.

10 Click in the location where you want
the image to appear.

11 Click the **Home** tab.

12 Click **Paste**.

The image appears in your document.

● You can click ⊠ to close the Clip Art
task pane.

SEARCH FOR CLIP ART IMAGES

1 Click in your document where you want to place an image.

2 If you closed the Clip Art task pane, complete Steps **1** to **3** in the subsection "Copy Images from the Clip Organizer Window."

3 Click here and type one or more words to describe the image you want to find.

4 Click **Go**.

A message may appear, asking if you want to search online; click **Yes** or **No**, as appropriate.

Note: This example does not search online.

● Images matching the words you typed appear here.

5 Click an image.

● The image appears in your document with ⊡ and ⊡ surrounding the image.

● Picture Tools appear on the Ribbon.

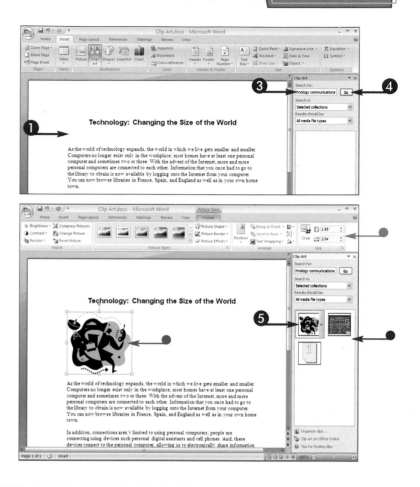

What happens if I click the Search in ☑?

You have the opportunity to limit the search to specific collections. Searching will take less time if you limit the search, but the search may not display as many clip art images if you limit it.

What is a collection?

A *collection* is a group of clip art images that are related. Office Collections contains clip art images available on your hard drive or on your Office CD. Web Collections contains images available at Microsoft Office Online; you must be connected to the Internet to use Web Collections.

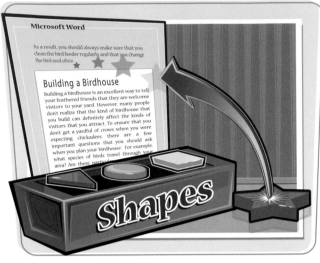

To give your Word document pizzazz, you can add graphic shapes such as lines, arrows, stars, and banners.

Shapes are visible only in Print Layout, Web Layout, and Reading Layout views. The remaining sections of this chapter show you how to use these tools to work with shapes.

Add a Shape

① Click the **Insert** tab.

② Click **Shapes**.

The Shapes Gallery appears.

③ Click a shape.

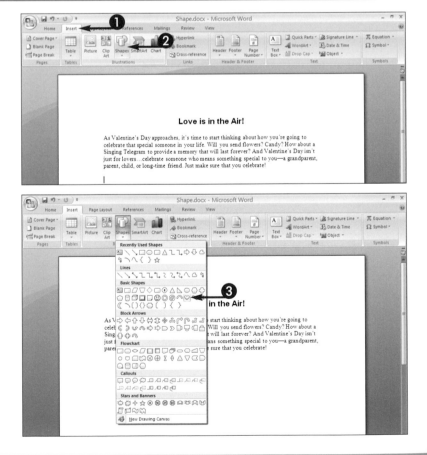

④ Position the mouse pointer at the upper left corner of the place where you want the shape to appear.

⑤ Drag the shape mouse (+) down and to the right until the shape is the size you want.

When you release the mouse button, the shape appears.

● The sizing handles (▢) that surround the shape indicate that the shape is selected.

● Drawing Tools appear on the Ribbon.

You can press Esc or click anywhere to continue working in your document.

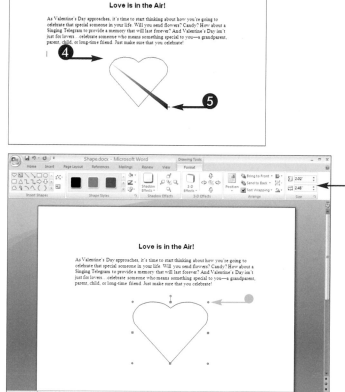

TIP

Can I place text inside a shape?

Yes, and when you do, Word converts the shape to a text box, as discussed in the section, "Add a Text Box."

① Click the shape to select it.

② Click **Drawing Tools** to display the Format tab.

③ Click the **Edit Text** icon (▤).

Word converts the shape to a text box, changing Drawing Tools to Text Box tools, and you can begin typing text inside the shape.

You can add a text box, which is another type of graphic, to your document to control the placement and appearance of the text that appears in the box.

Text boxes are visible only in Print Layout, Web Layout, and Reading Layout views.

① Click the **Insert** tab.

② Click **Text Box**.

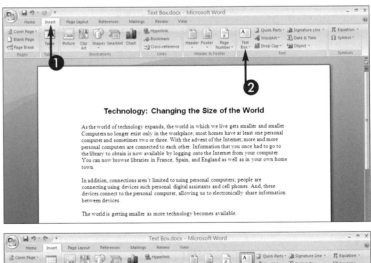

The Text Box Gallery appears.

③ Click a text box style.

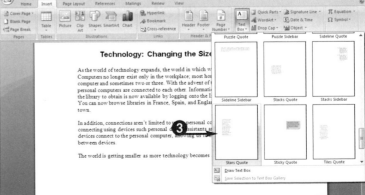

- Word places a text box in your document.
- Existing text flows around the box.

Sample text appears inside a Pull Quote box where you can type your text.

4 Position the mouse pointer inside the text box over the sample text and click.

Word selects the sample text.

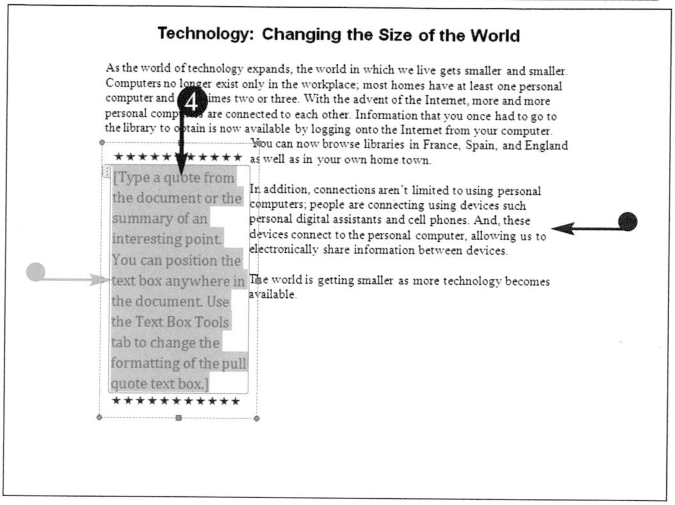

5 Type your text.

6 Click outside the text box.

Your text appears in the box using the predefined formatting of the text box style you selected in Step **3**.

***Note:** You can format the text using the techniques described in Chapter 5.*

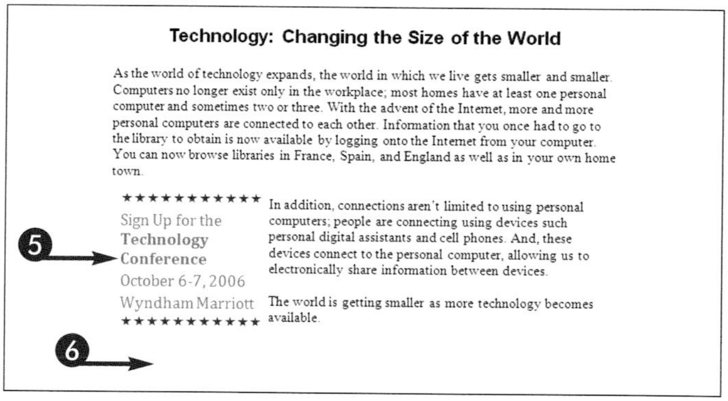

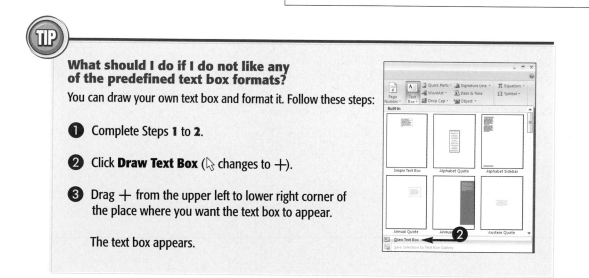

TIP

What should I do if I do not like any of the predefined text box formats?

You can draw your own text box and format it. Follow these steps:

1 Complete Steps **1** to **2**.

2 Click **Draw Text Box** (⇖ changes to +).

3 Drag + from the upper left to lower right corner of the place where you want the text box to appear.

The text box appears.

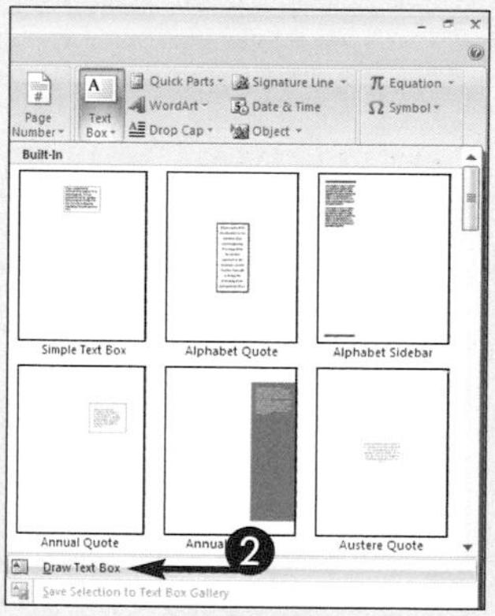

Move or Resize a Graphic

If you find that a graphic — a picture, ClipArt image, shape, text box, or WordArt graphic — is not positioned where you want it or if it is too large or too small, you can move or resize it.

MOVE A GRAPHIC

① Click the graphic.

● Handles (□, □, or ■) surround the graphic.

② Position the mouse pointer over the WordArt image, picture ClipArt image, or shape, or over the edge of the text box (I changes to ↔ or ✥).

③ Drag the graphic to a new location.

● A dashed line may appear, indicating the new location of the graphic.

The graphic appears in the new location.

④ Click outside the graphic to cancel its selection.

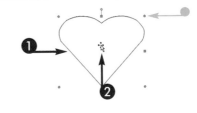

RESIZE A GRAPHIC

1 Click the graphic.

● Handles (◻, ▢, or ■) surround the graphic.

2 Position the mouse pointer over one of the handles (⊥ changes to ↗, ↔, ↘, or ↕).

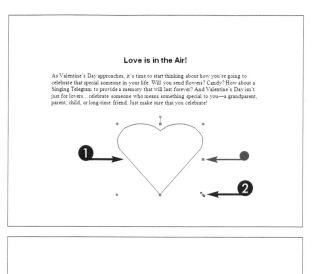

3 Drag the handle until the graphic is the appropriate size (↗, ↔, ↘, or ↕ changes to ┼).

● A dashed line indicates the new size of the graphic.

The graphic appears in the new size.

4 Click outside the graphic to cancel its selection.

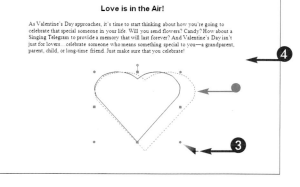

 TIPS

Is there an easy way I can make a graphic move only horizontally or vertically but not diagonally?

Yes. Press and hold the **Shift** key as you drag the graphic. Word allows you to move the graphic horizontally or vertically but not diagonally.

Does it matter which handle I use to resize a graphic?

If you click and drag any of the corner handles, you maintain the proportion of the graphic as you resize it. The handles on the sides, top, or bottom of the graphic resize the width or the height only of the graphic.

Rotate a Graphic

For dramatic effect, you can rotate pictures, clip art images, and some shapes. You cannot rotate text boxes.

Rotate a Graphic

① Click the image you want to rotate.

● Handles (◙, ◱, or ■) surround the graphic.

② Position the mouse pointer over the green handle at the top of the image (I changes to ↻).

③ Drag the mouse in the direction you want to rotate the image.

A dotted line marks the image position.

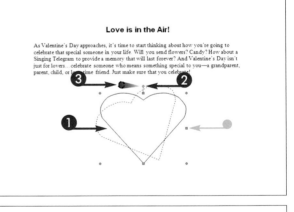

● Word displays the rotated image.

You can press Esc to cancel the selection of the image.

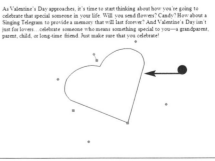

You can add color to a shape or a
text box to draw attention to it
or to make it more interesting.

Change the Color of a Shape

① Click the shape or text box to which you want to apply
color.

Handles (○) appear around the image.

② Click the **Format** tab for Text Box Tools or Drawing Tools.

③ Click the **Shape Fill** icon (🖌) to display available colors.

Note: Point the mouse at a color to preview the shape in the selected color.

④ Click the color you want to apply.

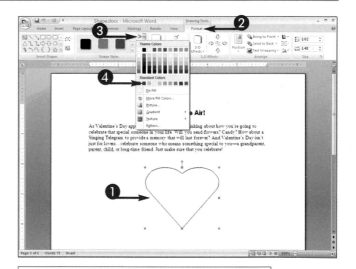

● Word fills the shape or text box with the selected color.

You can press **Esc** or click outside the image to
cancel the selection of the image.

Make a Shape Three-Dimensional

To create an interesting visual effect, you can make WordArt, a text box, or a shape appear three-dimensional.

You cannot make a picture or a clip art image appear three-dimensional.

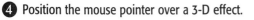

Make a Shape Three-Dimensional

1 Click a graphic.

Handles (■ or ◯) appear around the image.

2 Click the **Format** tab.

3 Click **3-D Effects**.

The 3-D Effects Gallery appears.

4 Position the mouse pointer over a 3-D effect.

● Live Preview displays the proposed effect, and the handles disappear.

5 Click a 3-D effect.

Word adds the three-dimensional effect to the graphic.

● To remove a three-dimensional effect, repeat Steps **1** to **5**, selecting **No 3-D Effect** in Step **5**.

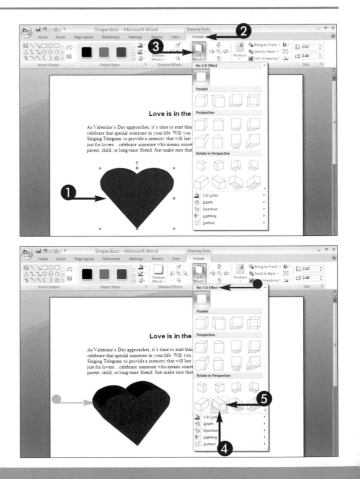

You can add depth to a picture, shape, WordArt image, or text box by adding a shadow to it.

You cannot add shadows to most clip art images.

Add a Shadow to a Shape

① Click a graphic.

Handles (■, ◯, or ▢) appear around the image.

② Click the **Format** tab.

③ Click **Shadow Effects**.

The Shadow Effects Gallery appears.

④ Position the mouse pointer over any shadow effect.

Live Preview displays the graphic in the proposed shadow effect, and the handles temporarily disappear.

⑤ Click a shadow effect.

● Word applies the shadow effect to the selected graphic.

To remove a shadow, repeat Steps **1** to **5**, selecting **No Shadow Effect** in Step **5**.

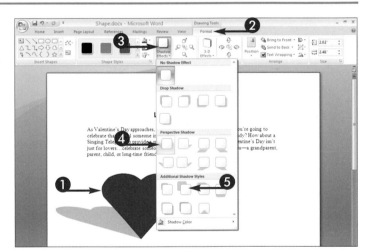

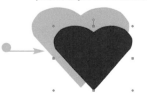

Apply a Style to a Shape

You can apply a predefined style to a shape, text box, WordArt graphic, picture, or Clip Art image. Styles help add interest to graphics.

Applying a style removes other effects you may have applied, such as shadow effects or 3-D effects.

Apply a Style to a Shape

① Click a graphic.

Handles (■, ▢, or ▢) appear around the image.

② Click the **Format** tab.

③ Click the **More** icon.

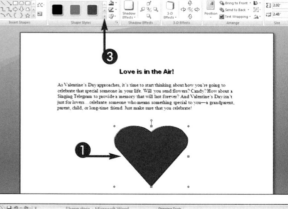

The Styles Gallery for the type of graphic you selected in Step **1** appears.

Note: This task displays the Shape Styles Gallery.

④ Position the mouse pointer over any style.

Live Preview displays the graphic in the proposed style, and the handles temporarily disappear.

⑤ Click a style.

● Word applies the style to the selected graphic.

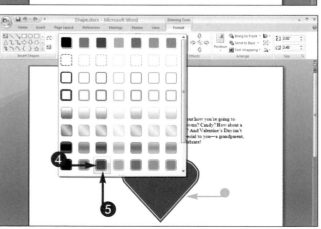

You can add color to the outline of a shape to which you have applied a style. This additional color can change the styled shape's appearance dramatically.

Color the Outline of a Styled Shape

1 Click a graphic.

Handles appear around the image.

2 Apply a style to the graphic.

Note: *See the section "Apply a Style to a Shape" for more information.*

3 Click here on the **Shape Outline** icon (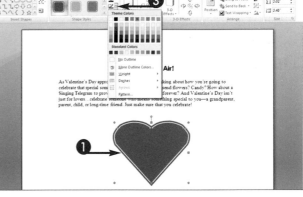).

The Shape Outline color gallery appears.

4 Position the mouse pointer over any color.

Live Preview displays the graphic outline in the proposed color.

5 Click a color.

● Word applies the color to the outline of the selected graphic.

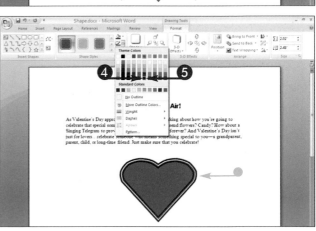

Understanding Text Wrapping and Graphics

When you insert graphics into a Word document, you can control the way that text wraps around the graphic. By default, most graphics you insert have a relatively square boundary, even if the graphic is not a square, and most text wrapping options relate to that relatively square boundary.

By editing a graphic's wrap points, you can change the square boundary to more closely match the graphic's shape and wrap text more closely around the shape.

Square
Wraps text in a square around your graphic regardless of its shape. You can control the amount of space between text and all your graphic's sides.

In Front Of Text
With this, the graphic blocks the text underneath the graphic's location.

In Line With Text
With this, text does not wrap around the graphic. Word positions the graphic exactly where you placed it. The graphic moves to accommodate added or deleted text, but no text appears on the graphic's right or left.

Behind Text
With this, the text runs over the graphic, as if the graphic were not there.

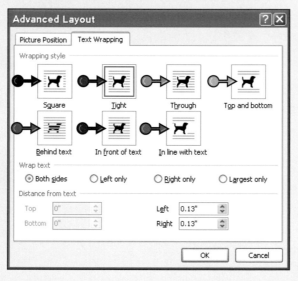

Top And Bottom
Wraps text around the graphic's top and the bottom, but leaves the space on either side of a graphic blank.

Tight
Wraps text around the graphic's outside edge. The difference between this and Square is apparent with a non-square shape; with Tight, you can control the space between the text and the graphic's right and left sides. Word leaves no space between text and the graphic's top and bottom sides.

Through
With Through, if you edit a graphic's wrap points by dragging them to match the shape of the graphic, you can wrap text to follow the graphic's shape.

Wrap Text Around a Graphic

You can control the way that Word wraps text around a graphic image in your document. This becomes very important when you want to place graphics in a document where space is at a premium, such as a two-columned newsletter.

The information in this section shows text wrapping for a shape but applies to text wrapping for any kind of graphic.

Wrap Text Around a Graphic

1 Click a graphic.

Handles (■, ○, or ▢) appear around the image.

2 Click the **Format** tab.

3 Click **Text Wrapping**.

4 Click the wrapping style you want to apply.

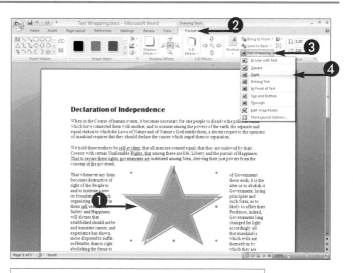

● Word wraps text around the graphic using the text wrapping option you selected.

Insert and Edit Diagrams

You can add an organization chart, or a cycle, radial, pyramid, Venn, or target diagram to your document to illustrate a concept.

The example in this section demonstrates adding an organizational chart.

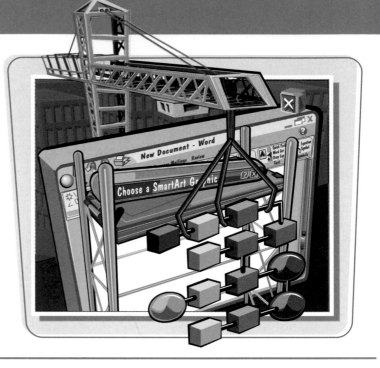

ADD A DIAGRAM

1 Click in your document where you want the diagram to appear.

2 Click the **Insert** tab.

3 Click **SmartArt**.

The Choose a SmartArt Graphic dialog box appears.

4 Click a diagram category.

5 Click the type of diagram you want to add.

● A description of the selected diagram appears here.

6 Click **OK**.

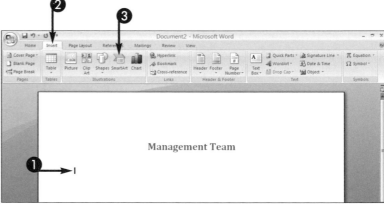

Word adds the diagram to your document.

● The graphic border surrounding the diagram indicates that the diagram is selected; the border will not print.

● SmartArt Tools appear on the Ribbon.

● The Text Pane appears here.

Each object within the diagram is called a *shape*.

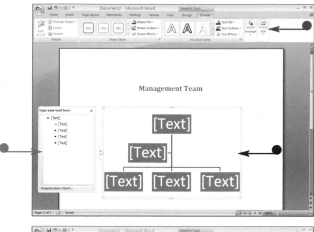

ADD TEXT TO THE DIAGRAM

7 Click next to a bullet in the Text pane.

● Handles (◻ and ▢) surround the shape associated with that bullet.

8 Type the text you want to add.

9 Repeat Steps **1** to **2** for each shape in the diagram.

● You can click **Text Pane** to hide or display the Text Pane as you need it.

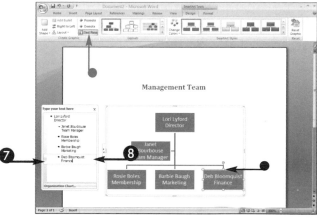

TIPS

How can I add two lines of text to a shape?

After you type the first line of the text in the Text pane, press **Shift** + **Enter** . Then, type the second line. Pressing **Enter** alone adds another shape to the diagram.

Can I control the size and position of the diagram on the page?

Yes. Click the **Format** tab, click **Size** and then click ⬍ to change the height and width. Word sets the default position on the diagram inline with your text. You can use the Position Gallery to place the diagram in one of nine predetermined positions on the page. Click **Arrange** and then click **Position** to display the Position Gallery.

continued

Insert and Edit
Diagrams *(continued)*

To keep your diagrams current and interesting, you can add or delete shapes and apply styles to diagrams.

ADD OR DELETE SHAPES

1 Click anywhere on the diagram to change the focus from the Text Pane to the diagram.

2 Click the shape above or beside where you want to add a shape.

● Handles (◯ and ▢) surround the shape you clicked.

3 Click ▼ below **Add Shape** and select the option that describes where the shape should appear.

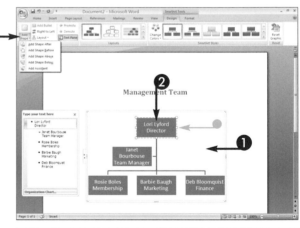

● The new shape appears.

You can add text to the new shape by following the steps in the subsection "Add Text to the Diagram" on the previous page.

APPLY A DIAGRAM STYLE

1 Click the **Design** tab.

2 Click here to display the Quick Styles Gallery.

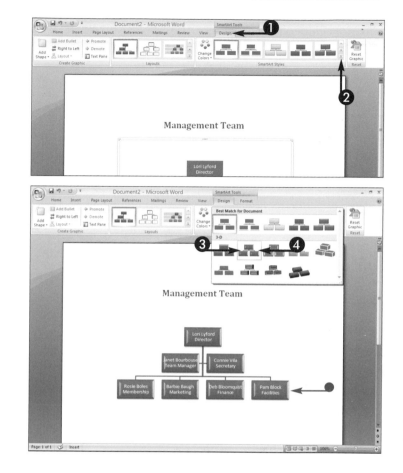

The Quick Styles Gallery appears.

3 Position the mouse pointer over a style.

Live Preview displays the diagram in the proposed style.

4 Click a style.

● Word applies the selected style to the diagram.

You can click anywhere outside the diagram to continue working.

TIPS

How can I delete a shape?
Click the shape; handles (□ and ▢) appear around the shape. Press the Delete key to remove the selected shape from the diagram.

Can I change the layout of an organization chart diagram after I insert it?
Yes. Click the organization chart to select it. Then, on the Design tab, click **Org Chart** to view your organization chart structure options.

Customize Word

Do you like the default Word settings? If not, you can easily customize portions of the Word program to make it perform more in line with the way you work.

Control the Display of Formatting Marks

Although you can display all formatting marks, you also can limit the formatting marks that Word displays to more clearly view your document.

Using the Show/Hide icon displays all formatting marks.

① Click the **Office** icon (🔘).

② Click **Word Options**.

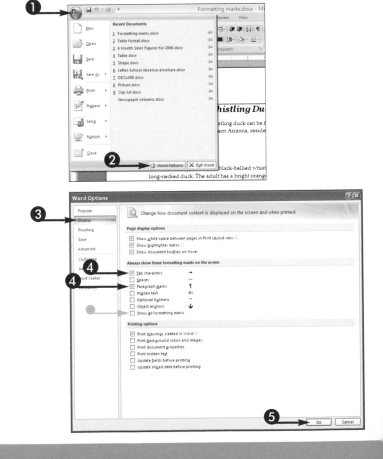

The Word Options dialog box appears.

③ Click **Display**.

● You can click the **Show all formatting marks** option (☑ changes to ☐) to display all formatting marks.

④ Click the formatting marks you want to display (☐ changes to ☑).

⑤ Click **OK**.

Word displays only the selected formatting marks in your document.

You can customize the status
bar to display information you
want visible while you work.

Customize the Status Bar

1 Right-click the Status bar.

Word displays the Status Bar
Configuration menu.

2 Click the option you want to display
on the status bar.

3 Repeat Step **2** for each option you
want to display.

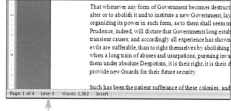

● Word displays the option you selected
on the status bar.

You can click anywhere outside the
menu to close it.

Work with the Quick Access Toolbar

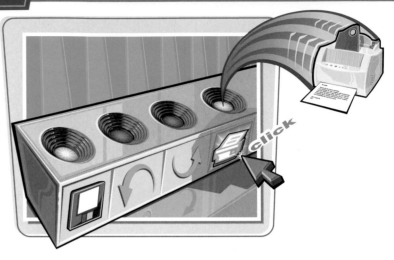

You can customize the Quick Access Toolbar in Word 2007 by changing both its appearance and its content.

Unlike previous versions of Word, you find only one toolbar, the Quick Access Toolbar in Word 2007.

Work with the Quick Access Toolbar

CHANGE PLACEMENT

① Click the **Customize Quick Access Toolbar** icon.

Word displays a menu of choices.

② Click **Show Below the Ribbon**.

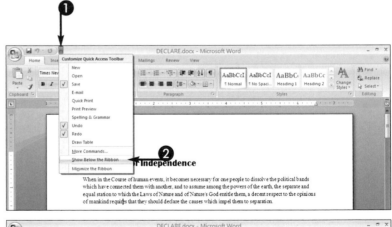

● The Quick Access Toolbar appears below the Ribbon instead of above it.

You can repeat these steps to move the Quick Access Toolbar back above the Ribbon.

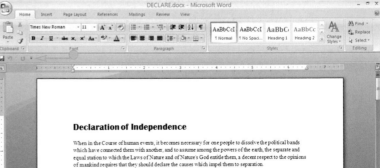

CUSTOMIZE THE QUICK ACCESS TOOLBAR

1 Click the **Customize Quick Access Toolbar** icon.

Word displays a menu of choices.

● You can click any command on the menu to add it to the Quick Access Toolbar.

2 Click **More Commands**.

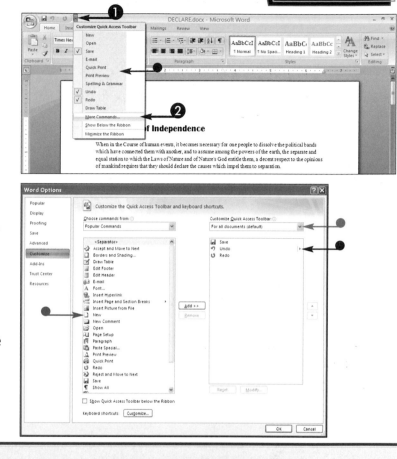

The Word Options dialog box appears, showing customization options.

● These commands, which you can add to the Toolbar, are associated with the menu that appears when you click the Office button.

● Commands already on the Toolbar appear here.

● You can use this list to customize the Quick Access Toolbar for all documents or just the current document.

TIP

Is there an easy way I can get rid of changes I made to the Toolbar?

Yes, you can reset it, by following these steps:

1 Perform Steps **1** to **2** in the subsection "Customize the Quick Access Toolbar."

2 Click **Reset**.

3 In the Reset Customizations dialog box, click **Yes**.

Word resets your Toolbar.

4 Click **OK**.

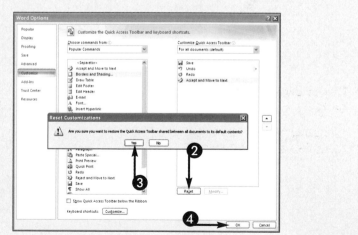

continued

You can add commands to the Quick Access Toolbar and reorganize the order in which commands appear on the Quick Access Toolbar.

Work with the Quick Access Toolbar *(continued)*

❸ Click here to display the various categories of commands.

At the bottom of the list, you can select **All Commands** to view all commands in alphabetical order regardless of category.

❹ Click a category of commands.

This example uses the File category.

❺ Click the command you want to add to the Toolbar.

❻ Click **Add**.

● Word moves the command from the list on the left to the list on the right.

❼ Repeat Steps **3** to **6** for each command you want to add to the Quick Access Toolbar.

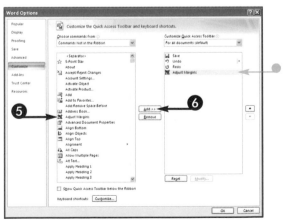

⑧ While viewing customization options in the Word Options dialog box, click a command in the right-hand column.

⑨ Click the **Move Up** icon (⬆) or the **Move Down** icon (⬇) to change a command's placement on the Quick Access Toolbar.

⑩ Click **OK**.

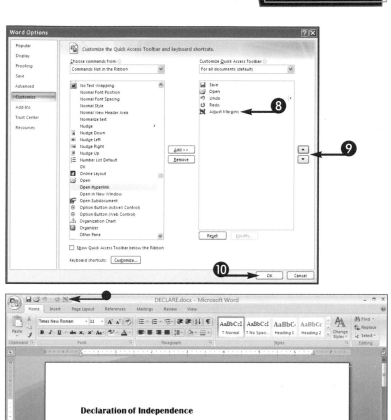

● The updated Quick Access Toolbar appears.

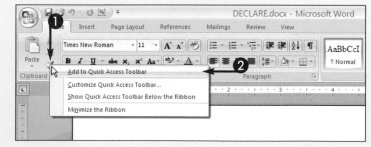

TIP

How do I add a button from the Ribbon to the Quick Access Toolbar?
Adding buttons from the Ribbon to the Quick Access Toolbar makes those buttons visible regardless of which Ribbon tab you view. You must still use the Word Options dialog box to change the order of the buttons.

① Right-click the button.

② Click **Add to Quick Access Toolbar**.

Word adds the button to the Quick Access Toolbar.

You can remove a button from the Quick Access Toolbar by right-clicking it and then clicking **Remove from Quick Access Toolbar**.

Add Keyboard Shortcuts

You can add keyboard shortcuts for
commands you use frequently.

**The appearance of the command on the Ribbon is not relevant;
you can create keyboard shortcuts for any command.**

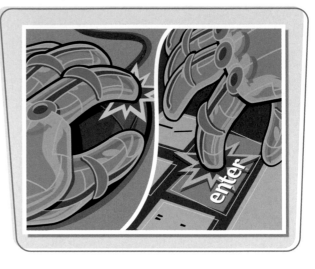

① Click 🔘.

② Click **Word Options**.

The Word Options dialog box appears.

③ Click **Customize**.

Customization options appear.

④ Click **Customize**.

The Customize Keyboard dialog box appears.

● Categories of commands appear here.

● Commands within a category appear here.

5 Click the category containing the command to which you want to assign a keyboard shortcut.

6 Click the command.

● Any existing shortcut keys for the selected command appear here.

7 Click here and press a keyboard combination.

● The keys you press appear here.

● The command to which the shortcut is currently assigned appears here.

8 Click **Assign**.

9 Click **Close**.

10 Click **OK**.

Word saves the shortcut.

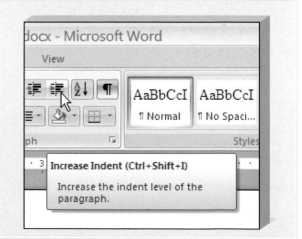

TIP

How can I test my shortcut to make sure it works?

You can press the keys you assigned. You also can position the mouse pointer over the tool on the Ribbon; assigned keyboard shortcuts appear in the ToolTip.

You can create a macro to save time. A macro combines a series of actions into a single command. For example, you can store repetitive text that you type frequently in a macro so that you can insert it quickly and easily.

You create a macro by recording the keystrokes that you use to take the action you want to store in the macro. In Word 2007, you initially need to enable macro recording.

ENABLE MACRO RECORDING

1. Click 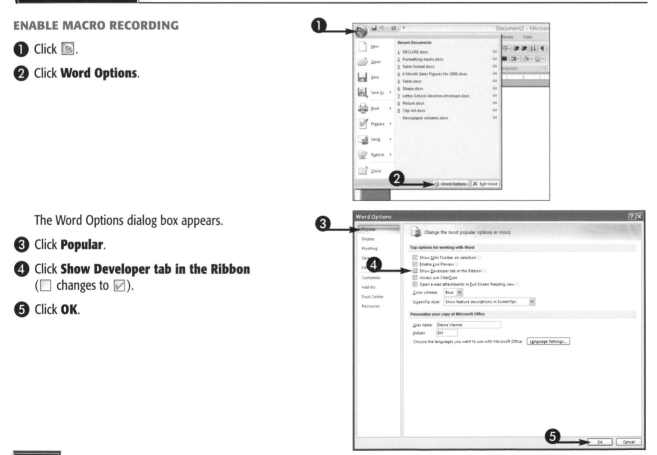.

2. Click **Word Options**.

The Word Options dialog box appears.

3. Click **Popular**.

4. Click **Show Developer tab in the Ribbon** (☐ changes to ☑).

5. Click **OK**.

● The Developer tab appears on the Ribbon.

RECORD A MACRO

① Click the **Developer** tab.

② Click **Record Macro**.

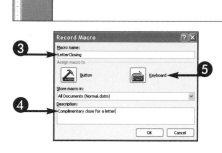

The Record Macro dialog box appears.

③ Type a name for the macro.

④ Type a description for the macro here.

⑤ Click **Keyboard**.

TIPS

Are there any rules I should follow when naming a macro?

Macro names must begin with a letter and contain no spaces. In addition, if you think you may want to view the macro code, you may find it easier to locate the macro if you name the macro something meaningful to you.

Do I need to re-create my macros from Word 2003?

No. If you upgrade from Word 2003, Word 2007 converts the Normal template you used in Word 2003. The converted Normal template contains all your macros, and they should appear in the Macros dialog box and work in Word 2007.

continued

By assigning the macro to a
keyboard shortcut, you can
quickly and easily run the macro.

Create a Macro *(continued)*

The Customize Keyboard dialog box appears.

6 Press and hold the **Alt** key and press a letter or number.

● The current assignment for the key combination you
selected appears here.

If anything other than [unassigned] appears, press
Backspace and repeat Step **6** using a different key
combination.

7 Click **Assign**.

● The key combination appears here.

8 Click **Close**.

- Stop Recording and Pause Recording become available on the Ribbon.

- The mouse pointer changes to ⌐.

⑨ Perform the actions you want included in the macro.

Note: *Macros can include typing, formatting, and commands. You cannot use the mouse to position the insertion point.*

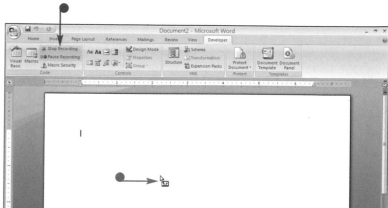

- You can click **Pause Recording** to temporarily stop recording and then click it again to resume recording.

⑩ Click **Stop Recording** when you have taken all the actions you want included in the macro.

Word saves the macro.

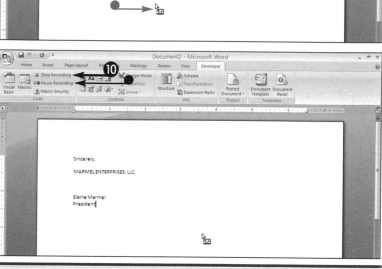

TIP

Can I assign a macro to the Quick Access Toolbar?

Yes. Use the following steps to assign the macro to the Quick Access Toolbar button instead of to a keyboard shortcut.

① Complete Steps **1** to **4** in the subsection "Record a Macro."

② Click **Button**.

③ In the Word Options dialog box, click the macro and click **Add**.

④ To rename the Toolbar button, click it and click **Modify** and type a new name here.

⑤ Click **OK** twice.

⑥ Complete Steps **9** to **10**.

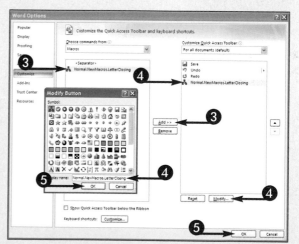

Run a Macro

You can run a macro to save time and let Word perform the actions stored in the macro. If you did not assign a keyboard shortcut or a Quick Access Toolbar button, you can use the steps in this section to run a macro.

To record a macro, see the section "Create a Macro."

Run a Macro

① Position the insertion point in your document where you want the results of the macro to appear.

② Click the **Developer** tab.

③ Click **Macros**.

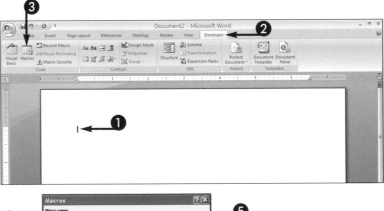

The Macros dialog box appears.

● Available macros appear here.

④ Click the macro you want to run.

● The macro's description appears here.

⑤ Click **Run**.

Word performs the actions stored in the macro.

Edit Macro Code

You can view macro code and make changes as needed.

For example, if you record a macro with a typographical error, you can correct the error.

Edit Macro Code

① Click the **Developer** tab.

② Click **Macros**.

The Macros dialog box appears.

③ Click the macro.

④ Click **Edit**.

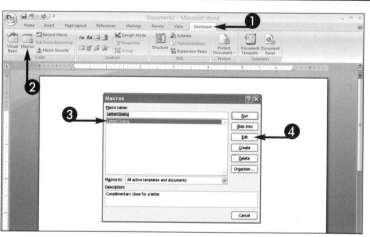

The macro code appears in a Visual Basic window.

⑤ Make changes as needed.

⑥ Click the **Close** icon (☒) to close the Visual Basic window.

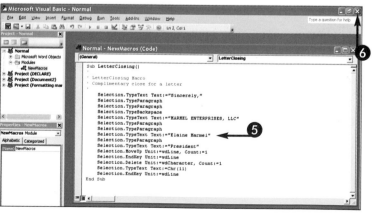

Work with Mass Mailing Tools

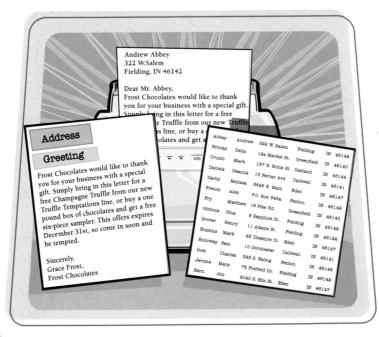

Why do the work yourself? You can use Word's mass mailing tools to create and mail form letters.

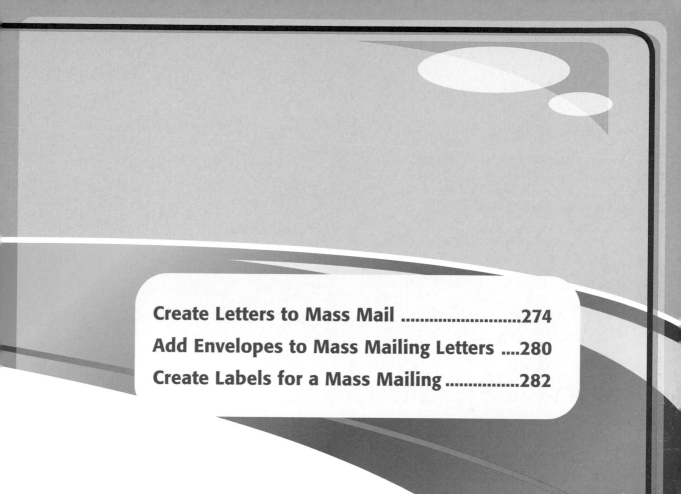

Create Letters to Mass Mail

Using a form letter and a mailing list, you can quickly and easily create a mass mailing that merges the addresses from the mailing list into the form letter.

Typically, the only information that changes in the form letter is the addressee information. You can create the mailing list as you create the mass mailing, or you can use a mailing list that exists in another Word document, an Excel file, or your Outlook Contact List.

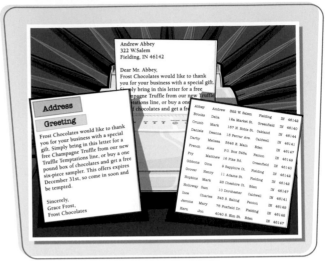

Create Letters to Mass Mail

1 Open the Word document that you want to use as the form letter.

Note: The letter should not contain any information that will change from letter to letter, such as the inside address.

2 Click the **Mailings** tab.

3 Click **Start Mail Merge**.

4 Click **Letters**.

Nothing happens on-screen, but Word sets up for a mail merge.

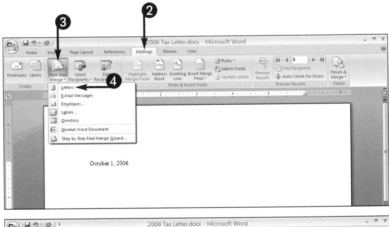

5 Click **Select Recipients**.

6 Click to identify the type of recipient list you plan to use.

This example uses an existing list in an Excel file.

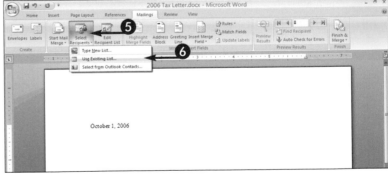

The Select Data Source dialog box appears.

7 Click here to navigate to the folder containing the mailing list file.

● You can use these buttons to navigate to commonly used folders.

8 Click the file containing the mailing list.

9 Click **Open**.

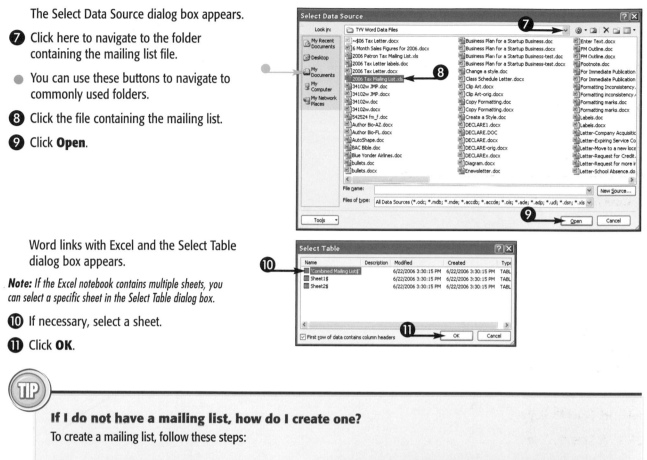

Word links with Excel and the Select Table dialog box appears.

Note: If the Excel notebook contains multiple sheets, you can select a specific sheet in the Select Table dialog box.

10 If necessary, select a sheet.

11 Click **OK**.

TIP

If I do not have a mailing list, how do I create one?
To create a mailing list, follow these steps:

1 In Step **6**, click **Type New List**.

2 In the New Address List dialog box, type recipient information, repeating Step **2** for each addressee.

3 Click **OK**.

4 Save the file in the Save Address List dialog box that appears, skipping to Step **12** in this section and finish the steps.

Note: See Chapter 2 for details on saving a file.

continued

275

You can select specific recipients from the mailing list to receive the form letter, and you use merge fields to specify the place in your document where the recipient's address and greeting should appear.

Create Letters to Mass Mail *(continued)*

⑫ Click **Edit Recipient List**.

The Mail Merge Recipients window appears.

● A check box (☑) appears beside each person's name, identifying the recipients of the form letter.

⑬ Click beside any addressee to whom you do not want to mail a form letter (☑ changes to ☐).

⑭ Click **OK**.

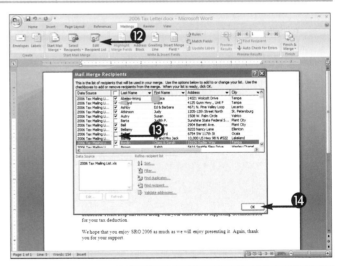

⑮ Click the location where you want the inside address to appear in the form letter.

⑯ Click **Address Block**.

The Insert Address Block dialog box appears.

⑰ Click a format for each recipient's name.

● You can preview the format here.

⑱ Click **OK**.

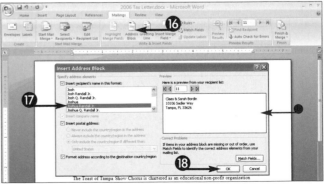

● A merge field representing the address block in the letter appears.

⑲ Click in the location where you want the greeting to appear.

⑳ Click **Greeting Line**.

The Insert Greeting Line dialog box appears.

㉑ Click here to specify the greeting format.

● A preview of the greeting appears here.

㉒ Click **OK**.

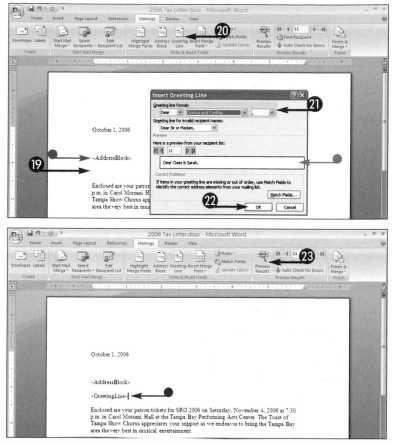

● A merge field representing the greeting line appears in the letter.

Note: *When you complete the merge, Word replaces the merge field with greeting information.*

㉓ Click **Preview Results**.

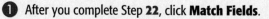

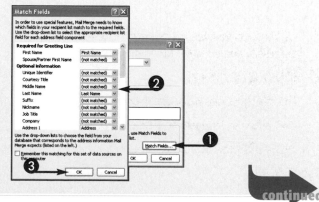

TIP

How do I know that Word will assign the correct fields in my mailing list file to the recipient's address information?

To make sure that Word assigns the correct fields, follow these steps:

❶ After you complete Step **22**, click **Match Fields**.

The Match Fields dialog box appears.

❷ Beside each field you use in your merge, click the ⌄ and select the corresponding field name in your mailing list file.

❸ Click **OK** and continue with Step **23**.

Word matches your fields.

continued

After you finish adding merge fields, you can preview the letters, select specific recipients and then create individual letters for each person in the mailing list file.

You also can merge the letters directly to your printer by creating an electronic file of letters. And, you can send the letters as e-mail messages.

- Word displays a preview of the merged letter, using the unchanging content of the letter and information from the address file.

- You can click the **Next Record** icon (▣) to preview the next letter and the **Previous Record** icon (▣) to move back and preview the previous letter.

- You can click **Preview Results** to redisplay merge fields.

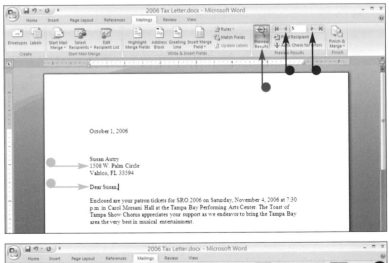

㉔ Click **Finish & Merge**.

㉕ Click **Edit Individual Documents**.

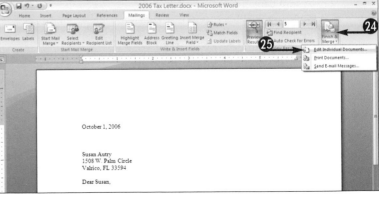

The Merge to New Document dialog box appears.

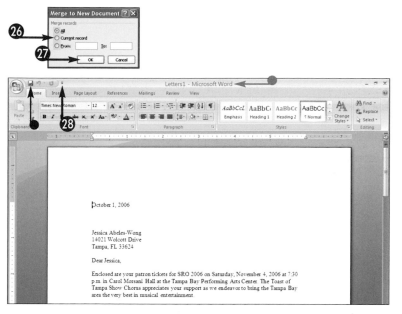

26 Click an option to identify the recipients of the letter (○ changes to ⦿).

The **All** option creates a letter for all entries on the mailing list; the **Current record** option creates only one letter for the recipient whose letter you are previewing; and the **From** option creates letters for recipients you specify.

27 Click **OK**.

● Word merges the form letter information with the mailing list information, placing the results in a new document named Letters1.

The new document contains individual letters for each mailing list recipient.

28 Click the **Customize Quick Access Toolbar** icon and click **Quick Print** from the list that appears.

● You can click 🖫 and assign a new name to save the merged letters.

What does the Auto Check for Errors button on the Ribbon do?

When you click this button, Word gives you the opportunity to determine whether you have correctly set up the merge. The Checking and Reporting Errors dialog box appears; click an option (○ changes to ⦿) and click **OK**. Depending on the option you choose, Word reports errors as they occur or in a new document.

Add Envelopes to Mass Mailing Letters

You can add addressed envelopes for letters you create using the Mail Merge feature in Word.

1 Create letters for the envelopes.

Note: *See the section "Create Letters to Mass Mail" for more on creating letters.*

2 On the Windows Taskbar, click the form letter you used to create the merged letters.

● Word displays the letter you set up to create the mail merge.

Note: *This example shows text not in Preview mode; click Preview Results to toggle Preview mode on and off.*

3 Click **Envelopes**.

The Envelopes and Labels dialog box appears.

4 Click **Add to Document**.

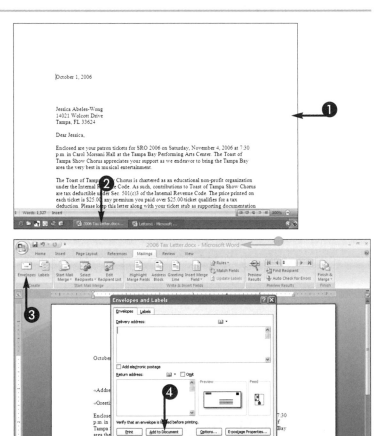

An envelope appears in your document.

5 Click in the center of the envelope to locate the address box.

● Dotted lines indicate the address box.

6 Click **Address Block**.

The Insert Address Block dialog box appears.

7 Click an address format.

8 Click **OK**.

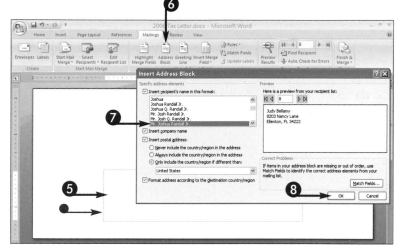

● A merge field appears on the envelope.

9 Follow Steps **23** to **28** in the preceding section, "Create Letters to Mass Mail," to preview envelopes, merge address information on envelopes, and print envelopes along with your letters.

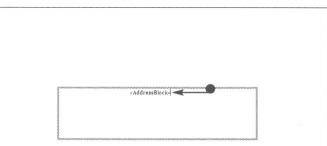

TIP

My printer does not have two trays, so I cannot print two different paper sizes at the same time, which the technique in this section requires. Can I still create envelopes for my letters?

Yes. Start in a blank document and follow the steps in the section "Create Letters to Mass Mail," but in Step **4**, click **Envelopes**. The Envelope Options dialog box appears. Select your envelope size and click **OK**. Then complete Steps **5** to **28**.

Create Labels for a Mass Mailing

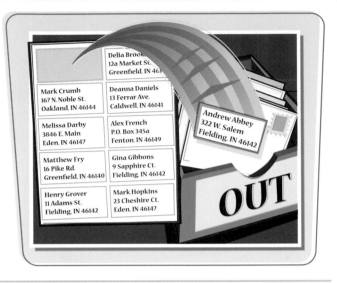

In addition to creating personalized form letters for a mass mailing, you can use the merge feature to create mailing labels for mass mailing recipients.

① Start a new blank document.

Note: See Chapter 2 for details starting a new document.

② Click the **Mailings** tab.

③ Click **Start Mail Merge**.

④ Click **Labels**.

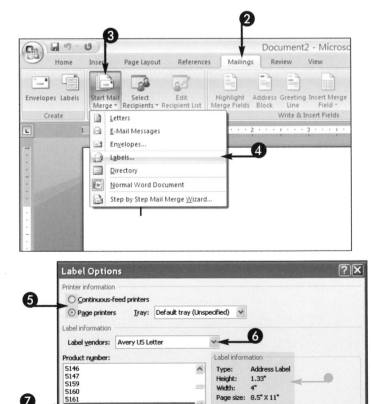

The Label Options dialog box appears.

⑤ Click an option to select the type of printer (○ changes to ⊙).

⑥ Click here to select a label product.

⑦ Click the label's product number.

● Information about the label dimensions appears here.

⑧ Click **OK**.

Word sets up the document for the labels you selected without gridlines to identify individual labels.

Note: To display gridlines, click the Layout tab and then click Show Gridlines.

⑨ Click **Select Recipients**.

⑩ Click to identify the type of recipient list you plan to use.

This example uses an existing list in an Excel file.

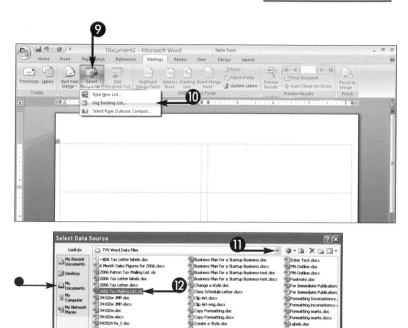

The Select Data Source dialog box appears.

⑪ Click here to navigate to the folder containing the mailing list file.

● You can use these buttons to navigate to commonly used folders.

⑫ Click the file containing the mailing list.

⑬ Click **Open**.

TIPS

What happens if I click Details in the Label Options dialog box?

A dialog box appears, displaying the margins and dimensions of each label, the number of labels per row, and the number of rows of labels, along with the page size. Although you can change these dimensions, you run the risk of having label information print incorrectly if you do.

What happens if I click New Label in the Label Options dialog box?

A dialog box appears. Word bases the appearance of this dialog box on the settings selected in the Label Options dialog box. You can use this dialog box to create your own custom label. Type a name for the label and then adjust the margins, height and width, number across or down, vertical or horizontal pitch, and page size as needed.

continued ➡

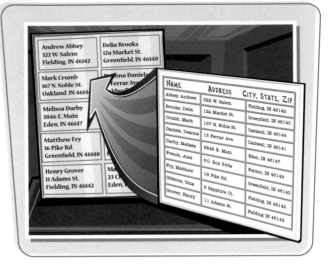

Using the label options you specify, Word sets up a document of labels to which you add merge information.

Word links with Excel and the Select Table dialog box appears.

Note: If the Excel notebook contains multiple sheets, you can select a specific sheet in the Select Table dialog box.

⑭ If necessary, select a sheet.

⑮ Click **OK**.

⑯ Click the first label where you want the first merge field to appear.

⑰ Click **Address Block**.

The Insert Address Block dialog box appears.

⑱ Click a format for each recipient's name.

● You can preview the format here.

⑲ Click **OK**.

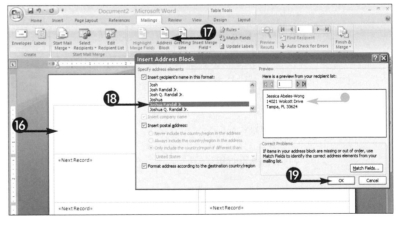

● Word adds the Address Block merge field to the first label.

Note: When you complete the merge, Word replaces the merge field with information from the mailing address file.

⑳ Click **Update Labels**.

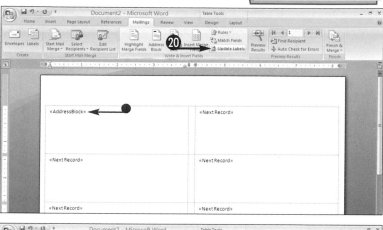

● Word adds the Address Block merge field to every label.

㉑ Click **Preview Results**.

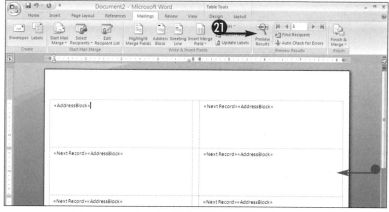

TIP

Can I selectively create labels using an existing file, or must I create labels for all recipients in the file?

You can select recipients. Follow these steps:

① Click **Edit Recipient List**.

The Mail Merge Recipients dialog box appears.

● A check box (☑) appears beside each person's name.

② Click beside any addressee for whom you do not want to create a mailing label (☑ changes to ☐).

③ Click **OK**.

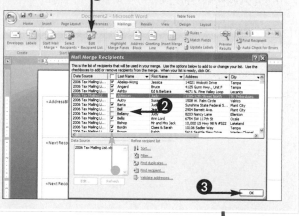

continued

You can preview the labels before you print them. When you complete the merge, you can merge all records in the mailing list file or only those you select.

Word displays a preview of your labels, replacing the merge field with information from the mailing list file.

● You can click ◀ to preview the next label and ▶ to move back and preview the previous label.

㉒ Click **Preview Results** to redisplay merge fields.

㉓ Click **Finish & Merge**.

㉔ Click **Edit Individual Documents**.

The Merge to New Document dialog box appears.

㉕ Click an option to identify the recipients of the letter (○ changes to ◉).

The **All** option creates a letter for all entries on the mailing list; the **Current record** option creates only one letter for the recipient whose letter you are previewing; and the **From** option creates letters for recipients you specify.

㉖ Click **OK**.

● Word creates the labels in a new Word document named Labels1.

The new document contains individual labels for each mailing list recipient.

㉗ Click the **Customize Quick Access Toolbar** icon and click **Quick Print** from the list that appears.

The labels print.

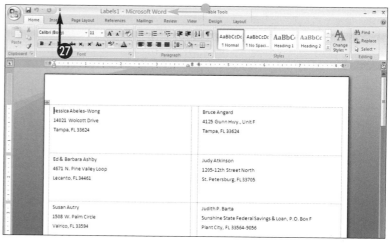

What happens if I click Finish & Merge and then click Print Documents?

The Merge to Printer dialog box appears. After you select the records you want to print, Word merges the information, allows you to select a printer, and then prints the merged label information without creating a separate document. This approach is useful if you know you do not need to make any changes to the labels.

If I merge to a document, should I save it?

Because you can re-create the merge whenever you need the labels, saving is not necessary. However, if you expect to print the labels often, you can save time if you save the labels.

CHAPTER 13

Word and the Internet

Using Word, you can interact with others over the Internet. You can e-mail a document, create a hyperlink in a document that will open a Web page or another document at your own site, and you can save a document as a Web page.

You can e-mail a Word document while you work in Word; you do not need to open your e-mail program and send the document from there. Word sends the document as an attachment.

Although you do not need to send the document from your e-mail program, your e-mail program must be set up on your computer.

E-mail a Document

① Open the document you want to send by e-mail.

② Click the **Office** icon (🔘).

③ Click **Send**.

④ Click **E-mail**.

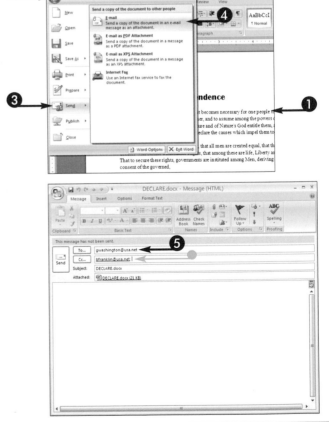

Word opens an e-mail message that you can address.

⑤ Click here to type the e-mail address of the person to whom you want to send the document.

● You can also type the e-mail address of someone to whom you want to send a copy of the message.

Note: *To send the message, or copies of the message, to multiple recipients, separate each e-mail address with a semicolon (;) and a space.*

6 Click here to type a subject for the e-mail message.

Note: Subjects are not required but including one is considerate. Word automatically supplies the document name for the subject; you can replace the document name with anything you want.

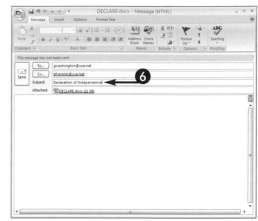

● You can type a message here.

7 Click **Send**.

Word places a message in your e-mail program's Outbox and closes the e-mail address.

Note: Your e-mail program must be open for the message to be sent.

TIPS

What should I do if I change my mind and do not want to send the document as an e-mail message?
Click ⊠ in the e-mail message window. A message appears, asking if you want to save the message. Click **No**.

Can I post a Word document as a blog?
Yes. Click 🔳, position the mouse pointer over **Publish**, and click **Blog**. You need a blog account; Word can help you find a blog provider if you click the Office Marketplace link in the Register a Blog Account window that appears.

Create a Hyperlink

Using a hyperlink, you can connect a word, phrase, or graphic image in a Word document to another document on your computer, or in your company's network, or to a Web page on the Internet.

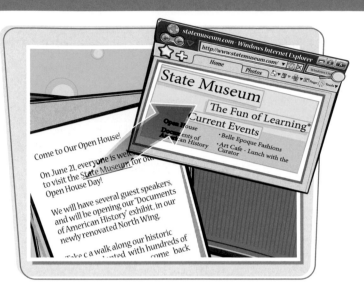

Create a Hyperlink

① Select the text or graphic you want to use to create a hyperlink.

② Click the **Insert** tab.

③ Click **Hyperlink**.

You can right-click the selection and click **Hyperlink** instead of performing Steps **2** to **3**.

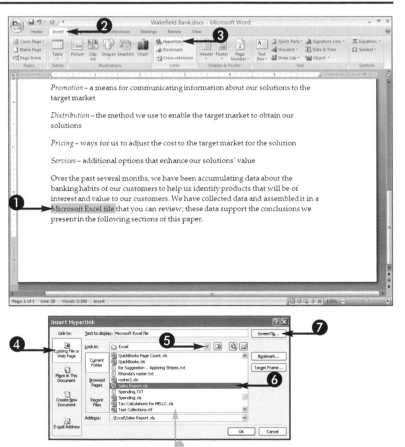

The Insert Hyperlink dialog box appears.

④ Click **Existing File or Web Page**.

● Files in the current folder appear here.

⑤ Click here and navigate to the folder containing the document to which you want to link.

⑥ Click the file to select it.

⑦ Click **ScreenTip**.

The Set Hyperlink ScreenTip dialog box appears.

8 Type text that should appear when a user positions the mouse pointer over the hyperlink.

9 Click **OK**.

The Insert Hyperlink dialog box reappears.

10 Click **OK**.

● Word creates a hyperlink shown as blue, underlined text in your document.

● The ScreenTip text appears when you position the mouse pointer over the hyperlink.

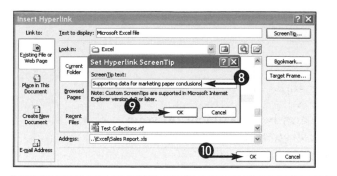

customers and for our organization, we use a diverse toolkit that focuses on:

Target Markets – those markets possessing needs we believe can be addressed by our marketing efforts.

Products/Services – a tangible or intangible solution to the target market's needs

Promotion – a means for communicating information about our solutions to the target market

Distribution – the method we use to enable the target market to obtain our solutions

Pricing – ways for us to adjust the cost to the target market for the solution

Services – additional options that enhance our solutions' value

Over the past several months, we have been accumulating data about the banking habits of ... Supporting data for marketing paper conclusions / Ctrl+Click to follow link ... collected data and assembled if in a Microsoft Excel file that you can review; these data support the conclusions we present in the following sections of this paper.

If I do not create a ScreenTip for the hyperlink, what appears when I position the mouse pointer over the hyperlink?

Word displays the location on your computer's hard disk or in your network, or, if you linked to a Web page, Word displays the Web address.

www.statemuseum.gov

How do I use a hyperlink that appears in a Word document?

Press and hold **Ctrl** as you click the hyperlink. The linked document or Web page will appear.

Save a Document as a Web Page

You can save any Word document as a Web page that you can then upload to the Internet.

Save a Document as a Web Page

1. Open the document you want to save as a Web page.

2. Click 🔲.

3. Point to **Save As**.

4. Click **Other Formats**.

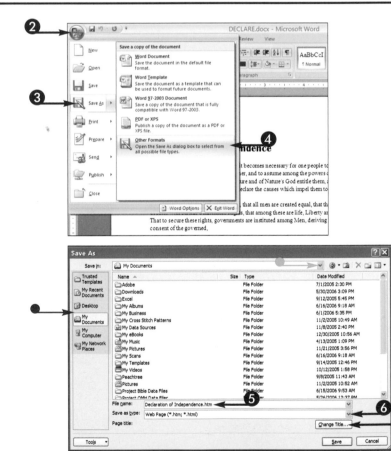

The Save As dialog box appears.

● The location where Word will save the file appears in the Save in dialog box; you can click here to save the Web page in a different location.

5. Type a name for the Web page here.

6. Click here and select **Web Page**.

● You can use these icons to navigate to commonly used locations.

7. Click **Change Title**.

The Set Page Title dialog box appears.

⑧ Type the title that you want to appear at the top of the screen when the page is displayed in a Web browser.

⑨ Click **OK**.

The Save As dialog box reappears.

⑩ Click **Save**.

● Word saves the document as a Web page and displays the document in Web Layout view, showing the document as it will appear in a Web browser.

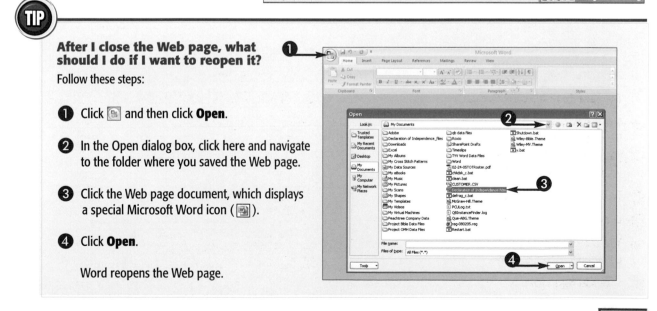

TIP

After I close the Web page, what should I do if I want to reopen it?

Follow these steps:

① Click ▣ and then click **Open**.

② In the Open dialog box, click here and navigate to the folder where you saved the Web page.

③ Click the Web page document, which displays a special Microsoft Word icon (▣).

④ Click **Open**.

Word reopens the Web page.

Index

Index

Index

Index

Undo feature
    delete text, 53
    undo changes, 55

V

View tab
    Document Map, 66
    Document Views, 64
    Thumbnails, 67
    Zoom, 68–69
views
    Draft view, 65
    Full Screen Reading view, 65
    Outline view, 65
    Print Layout view, 65
    switch between, 64
    Web Layout view, 65
Views icon, 23

W

watermark, 182–183
Web Layout view, 65
Web page, save document as, 294–295
widows, 159
width of columns in tables, 205

Word 97
    converting to Word 2007, 46–47
    save documents, 24
Word 2003, files saved in, 23
Word Count, 84–85
Word Options dialog box
    AutoCorrect Options, 86–87
    Check spelling as you type option, 92
    enable macro recording, 266
    keyboard shortcuts, 264–265
    Quick Access toolbar customization, 261
    Save AutoRecover information, 26
    show/hide formatting marks, 258
Word window, 5
WordArt, add, 230–231
WordArt Gallery, add WordArt, 230–231
words
    count in documents, 84–85
    select, 56
wrapping text. *See* text wrapping

X–Y–Z

X Y charts, description, 227
XPS documents, save in, 25

Zoom dialog box, 68–69
Zoom feature, 68–69

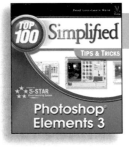

...all designed for visual learners—just like you!

Master VISUALLY®

Step up to intermediate-to-advanced technical knowledge. Two-color interior.

- 3ds max
- Creating Web Pages
- Dreamweaver and Flash
- Excel VBA Programming
- iPod and iTunes
- Mac OS
- Optimizing PC Performance
- Photoshop Elements
- QuickBooks
- Quicken
- Windows Server
- Windows

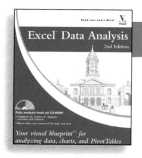

Visual Blueprint™

Where to go for professional-level programming instruction. Two-color interior.

- Excel Data Analysis
- Excel Programming
- HTML
- JavaScript
- PHP

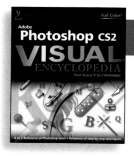

Visual Encyclopedia™

Your A to Z reference of tools and techniques. Full color.

- Dreamweaver
- Photoshop
- Windows

For a complete listing of Visual books, go to wiley.com/go/visualtech

Visual®
An Imprint of WILEY
Now you know.

Read Less–Learn More®

Visual™

Want instruction in other topics?

Check out these
All designed for visual learners—just like you!

0-470-04590-6

0-470-04573-6

0-7645-9640-3

**For a complete listing of *Teach Yourself VISUALLY*™ titles
and other Visual books, go to wiley.com/go/visual**

Visual®
An Imprint of ⊕**WILEY**
Now you know.